THE BLACKHAWKS

Also by Brian McFarlane

It Happened in Hockey

More It Happened in Hockey

Still More It Happened in Hockey

The Best of It Happened in Hockey

Stanley Cup Fever

Proud Past, Bright Future

It Happened in Baseball

The Leafs

The Habs

The Rangers

The Red Wings

The Bruins

THE BLACKHAWKS

BRIAN
MCFARLANE'S
ORIGINAL
SIX

BRIAN MCFARLANE

Published in 2000 by Stoddart Publishing Co. Limited
34 Lesmill Road, Toronto, Canada M3B 2T6
180 Varick Street, 9th Floor, New York, New York 10014

Distributed in Canada by:
General Distribution Services Ltd.
325 Humber College Blvd., Toronto, Ontario M9W 7C3
Tel. (416) 213-1919   Fax (416) 213-1917
Email cservice@genpub.com

Distributed in the United States by:
General Distribution Services Inc.
PMB 128, 4500 Witmer Industrial Estates,
Niagara Falls, New York 14305-1386
Toll-free Tel. 1-800-805-1083   Toll-free Fax 1-800-481-6207
Email gdsinc@genpub.com

04   03   02   01   00   1   2   3   4   5

Canadian Cataloguing in Publication Data

McFarlane, Brian, 1931–   .
The Blackhawks
(Brian McFarlane's original six)
ISBN 0-7737-3252-7

1. Chicago Blackhawks (Hockey Team) — History — Anecdotes.
I. Title. II. Series: McFarlane, Brian, 1931–   .
Brian McFarlane's original six.

GV848.C48M33 2000   796.962'64'0977311   C00-931296-X

U.S. Cataloguing in Publication Data
(Library of Congress Standards)

McFarlane, Brian.
The Blackhawks / Brian McFarlane. — 1st ed.
[240] p.: ill.; cm. (Brian McFarlane's Original Six)
Summary: Stories from seven decades of Blackhawks tradition.
ISBN 0-7737-32527

1. Chicago Blackhawks (Hockey team) — History. 2. Chicago Blackhawks
(Hockey team) — Anecdotes. 3. Hockey players — Biography. I. Title. II. Series.
796.962/64/ 0977 21 2000 CIP

Every reasonable effort has been made to obtain reprint permissions.
The publisher will gladly receive any information that will help rectify,
in subsequent editions, any inadvertent omissions.

Cover design: Bill Douglas @ The Bang
Text design and typesetting: Kinetics Design & Illustration

THE CANADA COUNCIL | LE CONSEIL DES ARTS
FOR THE ARTS | DU CANADA
SINCE 1957 | DEPUIS 1957

*We acknowledge for their financial support of our publishing program the Canada Council, the Ontario Arts
Council, and the Government of Canada through the Book Publishing Industry Development Program (BPIDP).*

Printed and bound in Canada

*To the gallant, gritty Chicago Blackhawks
who won the Cup in 1961, ending
Montreal's bid to win six consecutive
Stanley Cups*

Contents

1

Hockey Breezes into the Windy City

2

The First Golden Era

3

Hard Times on West Madison Street

4

Norris and Wirtz Take Charge

Muldoon's Curse Is Lifted

Close, But No Championships

7

The Hawks Rebuild

8

A Decade of Instability

Foreword

Many of my fondest memories of my NHL career are from the ten years I spent tending goal for the Chicago Blackhawks. I was blessed with wonderfully talented teammates in those days — Bobby and Dennis Hull, Stan Mikita, Pierre Pilote, Bill Hay, Eric Nesterenko, Moose Vasko, and many others. I think most fans will agree that during the sixties, Chicagoans who faithfully attended games at the old Chicago Stadium were entertained by the most exciting hockey in the team's long history.

In that era, it seemed that Bobby and Stan were always battling for individual scoring honors in the NHL, and three times they finished one-two among the league's top scorers. In 1967–68, Stan won three major trophies in one season — the Art Ross, the Hart, and the Lady Byng. And he came right back the following year to win all three again — a remarkable achievement.

And Bobby — the Golden Jet — was the league's most dazzling goal scorer in those days, and the game's most colorful player. He finished his NHL career with 610 goals. Who among us then would have predicted that his son Brett would someday surpass that amazing total?

Somewhere in the pages ahead, I known Brian will be writing about my consecutive games record of 502, which ended early in the 1962–63 season, but I hope he won't make it sound too special. Remember, goaltenders were expected to play in almost all the games back then and I have never thought the streak was all that remarkable. I say individual records should always take a back seat to a team accomplishment such as winning the Stanley Cup.

I was never so proud and happy as when the Hawks — third-place finishers behind Montreal and Toronto in 1960–61 — confounded the experts by capturing the Cup that spring. One game in the semifinals against Montreal required three overtime periods before Murray Balfour's goal won it for us. In game four, the Habs took 60 shots at me, 52 of them in the first two periods, and we lost, 5–2. My, how those Habs could skate and shoot. But somehow, thanks to my teammates, we managed a pair of shutouts in the next two games and eliminated the Canadiens, a team that had finished 17 points ahead of us.

In the final series against Detroit, we were deadlocked at two wins apiece when our goal scorers came through for us, outscoring the Wings 11–4 in the final two games and, for the first time since 1938, Chicago players sipped champagne from the Stanley Cup.

What a sweet feeling! There is no sense of accomplishment quite like it.

While the Hawks appear to be a long way from another Cup triumph, the game's history is full of dramatic turnabouts. Let's hope that Hawk fans, fans I remember fondly because they were always so hopeful, knowledgeable, and supportive, will see their team rise to the top again soon.

Glenn Hall
June 2000

Acknowledgments

T HE author wishes to thank the following contributors to *The Blackhawks*, the sixth and final book in the Original Six series: Steve Dryden, editor-in-chief of *The Hockey News*, for permission to use excerpts from his popular publication; Paul Patskou, Brian Beattie, Normand Pawluck, Eric Anderson, and Sally Karam for their research and writing contributions; Dennis Hull, Bill White, Bob Pulford, Glenn Hall, Gus Bodnar, Harry Watson, Eddie Litzenberger, Carl Brewer, Russ Conway, and Dick Irvin for their reminiscences, fact-checking wizard Ron Wight for his input; and two special friends at Stoddart, Jim Gifford and Don Bastian.

1

Hockey Breezes into the Windy City

Birth of the Blackhawks

MOST of the 5,000 sports fans who attended the Chicago Blackhawks' on-ice debut on November 17, 1926, had never seen a hockey game before. Many of the attendees held high social positions in the city — department-store king Marshall Field, for example — and they were there for two reasons: they had heard the game was fast, rough, and exciting; and they were willing supporters of the various charities that would share in the gate receipts.

Earlier in the day, the city's elite had attended a luncheon of the Union League Club, where they greeted a famous visitor to Chicago — Queen Marie of Romania. Major Frederic McLaughlin, owner of the Blackhawks, was hopeful that she would make an appearance at the game that night — imagine having a Queen drop the puck for the first-ever face-off in Blackhawk history! — but Her Majesty was a no-show.

Major McLaughlin had made his fortune in the coffee business — McLaughlin's Manor House Coffee was a favorite with housewives across America. He was also a sportsman, said to be one of the most skilful polo players in North America. Among his friends was the noted sports entrepreneur from New York, Tex Rickard, who a few months earlier had established an NHL team of his own, the New York Rangers. It was Rickard who suggested that McLaughlin consider buying a franchise for Chicago. "Think of the great rivalry we can develop," Rickard told McLaughlin.

McLaughlin thought the franchise fee of $12,000 was a bargain. He liked the speed and harsh body contact the game provided. He quickly formed a syndicate of more than a hundred friends, wrote out a check, and almost overnight became an owner of one of the ten teams that then comprised the NHL. He counted himself lucky to be welcomed into the lodge because two other parties had shown interest in landing the Chicago franchise.

Imagine the Major's delight when his Hawks, playing before a full house of shrieking fans, many of whom would become lifelong addicts to the game, defeated the visiting Toronto St. Pats in the first game by a 4–1 score.

A newspaper account of that opening was, by today's standards, overly wordy, a puzzle to read, and tardy in reporting the final score. The opening paragraph read as follows:

> Professional hockey under league auspices was ushered in here under most propitious circumstances last night, the Coliseum being crowded to capacity by a cheering throng who went away supremely happy because the Chicago Black Hawks made good their first time of asking at the expense of the Toronto St. Pats. The Rosebuds transplanted from Portland proved anything but bloomers taking kindly to their new surroundings and winning handily from the speedy Toronto team by 4–1. The victors had a nice margin on the play throughout no doubt due to the fact that they have had the benefit of several tidy tilts of an exhibition nature while the Queen City crowd were making their first appearance with colors up for the coming season.

McLaughlin was so pleased with the result that he voiced no criticism of the confounding prose that described his team's initial triumph.

McLaughlin had promised the Windy City fans he'd cough up a large part of his fortune to buy players for his club. The demise of the Western Hockey League at the end of the 1925–26 season had all the NHL franchises, new and old, scrambling to sign players who were anxious to move east and resume their careers in the NHL. McLaughlin boldly purchased the entire roster of the Portland Rosebuds from Frank and Lester Patrick for $150,000.

The prize in the package was forward Dick Irvin, a future Hall of Famer who had scored 31 goals in 30 games to tie Bill Cook for Western League scoring honors in '25–26. Irvin would be named the first captain of the Blackhawks and would finish second in league scoring with 18 goals and 18 assists. When a fractured skull ended his playing career in 1929, he turned to coaching and, at the helm of the Blackhawks, Toronto Maple Leafs, and Montreal Canadiens, he would set a long-lasting NHL record for coaching wins.

Dick Irvin, Jr., the noted Canadian hockey broadcaster, tells an amusing story about his father's coaching renown. Some time ago, a Chicago journalist called the Irvin home in Montreal.

"Mr. Irvin," said the voice on the phone, "I wonder if you could tell me what it was like for you to coach the Chicago Blackhawks in the late 1920s?"

Irvin, Jr., laughed and responded, "The man who could tell you, if he were still around, would be about 110 years old now."

Prior to the 1926–27 season, the NHL governors decided to operate with two divisions, the Canadian and the American. The former included the Montreal Canadiens, Montreal Maroons, Toronto St. Patricks (who changed their name to the Maple Leafs later that season), Ottawa Senators, and, oddly enough, the New York Americans. The American Division consisted of the Blackhawks, New York Rangers, Boston Bruins, Pittsburgh Pirates, and Detroit Cougars (eventually the Red Wings). The Bruins had been around for a couple of seasons, and Pittsburgh had one year under its belt. The other three clubs in the division were complete newcomers.

After much deliberation, McLaughlin chose the name Black Hawks (now Blackhawks) for his team. Some say he selected the name because he served as commander of the 333rd Machine Gun Battalion of the Eighty-fifth (Blackhawk) Division during World War I. The division's nickname commemorated Blackhawk, a famous Midwestern Indian chief of the nineteenth century. Others say McLaughlin named his team after a Chicago restaurant he owned called the Blackhawk. There's probably some truth in both stories.

Oddly, until 1986, the team name was always written as two

words — Black Hawks. That year, owner Bill Wirtz decided to change the spelling to conform to Chicago's original NHL charter of 1926. For six decades, the name had been misspelled on thousands of pieces of correspondence, team scoresheets, and publicity handouts.

When it came time to design the team uniforms, the Major's wife volunteered to help out. She was the former Irene Castle, a famous dancer and actress, and McLaughlin was quick to say "Yes, dear" when she suggested a colorful depiction of an Indian chief for the front of the new uniforms.

The Blackhawks' first home was the 5,000-seat Chicago Coliseum, a building often used for cattle shows. Those early games were attended by wealthy Chicagoans, many of them friends of McLaughlin's. Out of respect for the Major, few of them ever dared suggest that the lingering odor in the building might be caused by the performance of the home team, struggling through another game on the ice.

Muldoon's Irish Curse

IN 1926, Pete Muldoon became the first of many coaches Frederic McLaughlin would hire to run his Blackhawks over the years. Muldoon guided his new team to a third-place finish in the American Division and thought he'd done a commendable job with the talent placed at his disposal. He was proud of the fact his Hawks had scored 115 goals — more than any other NHL club.

If he expected a pat on the back from the Major, he didn't get it. The impatient owner told Muldoon the Hawks should easily have finished in first place. Muldoon was fired on the spot and replaced by Barney Stanley.

"You SOB," Muldoon is reported to have said. "Why, I'll place an Irish curse on your club that'll keep them out of first place forever! You just wait and see."

The Major just laughed.

A decade went by, then another. And a third and a fourth. The Hawks suffered through many bad seasons and celebrated a few good ones. They won Stanley Cups in 1934, '38, and '61. But forty years later they still hadn't found their way to the top of the league standings.

From time to time, journalists and broadcasters would bring up Muldoon's hex, which certainly seemed to be working. In 1963 and '64 the Hawks came close, finishing just one point out of first each year. It wasn't until 1966–67 that Bobby Hull, Stan Mikita, & Company led Chicago to top spot in the NHL. That season they compiled 94 points, well ahead of second-place Montreal's 77. Major McLaughlin would never see the "Curse" lifted — he died in 1944.

But was there really a curse? In conversation with noted Canadian sports columnist Jim Coleman one day, I found the answer.

"Years ago I had a daily column to write," he told me. "I was a drinking man in those days and meeting a deadline was sometimes a bit of a problem."

An impish smile crossed his face. "With the blank page in the typewriter staring back at me, and my deadline looming, I concocted the story of Pete Muldoon and the strange curse he once placed on the Blackhawks. It was pure fiction and it filled a column. I figured it would be forgotten in a day or two. But years later, people kept referring to the famous Muldoon Curse as if it was fact. Especially when the Hawks appeared destined never to finish ahead of the pack.

"Maybe I should have had old Pete condemn the Hawks to last-place finishes. They managed to do that often enough — at least fourteen times."

Paddy Harmon's Legacy

MUCH of Paddy Harmon's life was wrapped up in the Chicago Stadium, so it was only appropriate that in death he rested there.

Who was Patrick T. "Paddy" Harmon? He was a promoter with a flair for showmanship and a well-known Chicago sportsman who almost became the owner of the city's NHL franchise in 1926.

When he heard the NHL was planning to expand, Harmon journeyed to Montreal, where he attended a meeting of the league governors. He casually tossed a black satchel onto the table and produced a roll of fifty $1,000 bills. "Gentlemen, this is what I'm willing to pay to become a member of your league, no more, no less. I believe it should be enough to get me the Chicago franchise."

What Paddy didn't know, and what the governors were forced to tell him, was that the Chicago franchise had been secretly granted to another Chicagoan, Major Frederic McLaughlin, for a mere $12,000. How glum the governors must have been when Harmon stuffed the bills back into the satchel.

Undaunted, Harmon returned to Chicago. McLaughlin may have captured the franchise, but he didn't own a major-league arena. Harmon decided to build one, and he planned to make it the largest arena used for hockey in North America.

Paddy Harmon had experienced all the highs and lows of a natural gambler, from his days as a corner newspaper boy to the completion of his crowning achievement, the building of the mammoth Stadium. He had money, which he'd amassed by promoting dance halls, boxing matches, and six-day bicycle races — you name it. And he pumped more than $2 million of his own cash into the Stadium project. The rest of the financing came from his pals, who'd been sweet-talked into backing Harmon's vision. Most turned out to be fair-weather friends who squeezed Paddy out of the picture unceremoniously a few months after the Stadium opened, leaving him penniless and no doubt heart-broken.

The $7 million structure, which opened to rave reviews with a boxing match on March 28, 1929, was destined to house every conceivable attraction, drawing millions of fans and spectators to sporting events, concerts, political conventions — even a National Football League championship game.

On July 22, 1930, accompanied by his wife and a friend, Harmon was returning to Chicago by automobile from his summer home in Crystal Lake, Illinois. Near Des Plaines — a Chicago suburb — his car hit a soft spot on the road. The speeding machine, estimated to be traveling at between 30 and 35 miles per hour, plunged off the road and flipped over five times, pinning its occupants beneath it.

Harmon, who suffered internal injuries, was rushed to a hospital, where he died of lung hemorrhaging three hours later. His wife and the friend survived.

Knowing he was dying, Harmon made a deathbed wish. Would someone please arrange to have his body rest in Chicago Stadium, the place he proudly considered home?

His wish was granted and hundreds of mourners passed by his coffin in the cavernous arena to pay their respects. The man who had been both rich and poor died with $2.50 in his pocket.

Herb Gardiner a Rare Gem

WHEN Frederic McLaughlin hired veteran defenseman Herb Gardiner to be the playing coach of the Blackhawks in 1928 he knew it was going to be a short-term association. Gardiner was on loan to the Hawks from the Montreal Canadiens, and before the 1929 playoffs rolled around the Habs decided they needed him back.

As it turned out, the husky Gardiner played in only 13 games as a Blackhawk. And his coaching record was a disaster, for in 1928–29 the Hawks won an all-time low 7 games and scored a mere 33 goals during the 44-game schedule. The opposition blanked them an incredible 20 times. No wonder the 37-year-old Gardiner was happy to skedaddle back to Montreal in time to play in the Stanley Cup playoffs.

If his last NHL season was one he'd rather forget, his debut had been truly remarkable. He had joined the Canadiens two years earlier, at the age of 35, and played so well that he captured the 1927 Hart Trophy as the NHL's most valuable player. If there'd been a Norris Trophy, he might have won that, and been a First-Team All-Star, too. It's hard to believe, but Gardiner had once spent eight years away from hockey. He'd been a member of a survey party for four years, then served another four in the Canadian army during World War I. He returned to the game at age 28, toiling in the Western Canada Hockey League for seven seasons before joining the NHL and becoming its brightest star.

Despite the fact that his NHL career lasted only a little more than two seasons (101 games), and that he performed with a Chicago club that was one of the worst in history, Gardiner was inducted into the Hockey Hall of Fame in 1958.

Goalie Lehman
Becomes a Coach

GOALTENDER Hughie Lehman, a native of Pembroke, Ontario, had almost two decades of professional hockey behind him — most of it in Western Canada — when he joined the Chicago Blackhawks for their inaugural season.

He played in all 44 games for the Hawks in 1926–27, but saw

action in a mere four games the following year. Lehman was ready to pack it in. He'd celebrated his 42nd birthday and the current season would soon be coming to a close. He decided he'd had enough. It was time to go home.

Before he returned to Canada, however, he dropped in to the Blackhawks' front office, where he found Major McLaughlin expounding his theories on hockey. The Major had an audience of several players and he was excitedly mapping out some fancy plays in chalk on the hardwood floor. The Major was an impatient owner. In less than two seasons, he'd already fired two coaches — Pete Muldoon and Barney Stanley — and it looked as if he was planning to take over the coaching reins himself, at least for the 21 games that remained in the season.

McLaughlin stood and beamed at his captive audience. He turned to Lehman and said, "Well, Hughie, what do you think of the plays I've invented?"

Lehman, with nothing to lose, laughed out loud. He said, "Boss, that is the damndest piece of nonsense I've ever seen in my life."

Having offered his opinion, he turned and walked out the door.

Later that day, when he was packing his bags in his hotel room, the telephone rang.

"Major McLaughlin wants to see you again before you leave," the owner's secretary said. "Can you come right over?"

"I can and I will," Lehman replied, "because the club still owes me my final paycheck."

When he arrived at the arena, he was escorted into the Major's posh office.

"Hughie, I've decided not to coach the team after all. I want you to do it."

Lehman was stunned. But he recovered quickly and told the Major he'd be delighted to accept the assignment. For the last half of the season he was the head coach of a team in the NHL. But the Blackhawks won only three games, and that wasn't good enough for McLaughlin. The mercurial owner called Lehman into his office once more — this time to tell him he'd been fired.

Godfrey's Grand Design

IN his first decade as owner of the Blackhawks, Major McLaughlin hired and fired ten coaches.

One of his short-term mentors was a chap named Godfrey Matheson, a man he met by chance during a train ride. Matheson's hockey credentials were rather sparse — few in pro hockey had ever heard of him — but McLaughlin was impressed with the fact that Matheson claimed to have guided a Midget team in Winnipeg to some sort of local championship.

"You're just the man to coach my Blackhawks," the startled Matheson was told.

Sportswriter Len Bramson painted a word picture of the new coach after his arrival:

> He was a studious, ascetic-looking chap. He herded the Hawks to Pittsburgh for training camp and on the first day he turned up wearing shin pads over his trousers, elbow pads around his knees, a cap with tassels on his head, and he carried two buckets of hockey pucks.
>
> The first practice was unique. Matheson kept flipping pucks on the ice and as the players skated by they shot them at the net. But he refused to let his goalie, Charlie Gardiner, go in the goal for fear he would get hurt by one of the flying pucks.
>
> Matheson then picked a team of six players — the fastest skaters and the best stickhandlers — and while the others sat on the bench he told them, "Men, this is my first team. You watch them play and pay attention to each individual so that you can adapt yourself to his style of play. Then, when I need you in a game, you'll fit right in."

For the rest of the camp, the first team did almost all of the training while the reserve players sat on the boards or on the bench, telling stories and making jokes, smoking cigarettes and doing little to get in shape.

Matheson's tactics during games were truly astonishing. For example, he directed Mush March, who at five-foot-five and 150 pounds was as big as a button, to carry the puck over the opposing team's blue line and try to split the defense. At the last second, March was to drop the puck to Taffy Abel, a 220-pound defenseman who would be right on his heels. Abel would then bull his way in and score a goal.

The novel strategy didn't work. March would hit the defense and be hammered into the ice and Abel, if he made it to the goal, never scored. In fact, he averaged fewer than two goals a season in five years as a Blackhawk.

Matheson's most remarkable innovation, one that left everyone on the ice and at rinkside bewildered, was his whistle-blowing system of coaching from the bench.

Matheson signaled plays by blowing a whistle. One blast meant the puck carrier should pass the puck, two blasts called for him to shoot on goal. Three toots and the players were to wheel and backcheck, and so on. It was the most bizarre coaching strategy ever conceived.

Even Vic Ripley, one of his first-teamers, said, "Believe it or not, I couldn't believe it."

The players found it impossible to react to all the whistles and some, no doubt wishing they'd worn earmuffs, ignored the coach altogether. Old-time reporters fail to mention whether or not this whistle-happy Winnipegger ever used his strategy in an actual game. If he did, one can only speculate on how long the referee would tolerate those piercing blasts from the greenhorn coach before the whistle would be pushed down his throat.

Perhaps this Stone Age Roger Neilson had other, more practical innovations he was planning to introduce, but we'll never know. After just two games, one of the shortest coaching careers in NHL history ended abruptly.

The Major told Matheson, "Pack your bags, take your damn whistle, and get the hell out of town."

2

The First
Golden Era

A Dummy in Goal

S any goaltender will tell you, you have to be a little brain-damaged to play between the pipes. Only a dummy would gleefully throw his torso in front of all those screaming slap shots. And once, in the long history of the National Hockey League, a bona fide dummy actually showed up as a practice goalie in the NHL, and it happened in Chicago.

In the early '30s, Blackhawks owner Frederic McLaughlin decided his team needed a second goaltender — one who had no fear of shooting drills; who never complained when high shots flew past his head or when he was knocked around in his crease; and best of all, one who never asked to be paid. When told that such fellows were extremely rare, especially when it came to performing gratis, McLaughlin decided to invent one.

McLaughlin had a staff member stuff bags filled with straw into a scarecrow-shaped figure that roughly resembled a goalie. After the dummy was thoroughly stuffed, it was hauled across the ice and strung up in the center of the net. During practice, while All-Star netminder Charlie Gardiner tended goal at one end of the ice, the dummy defended the opposite goal. Chicago players blistered their hardest shots at him, hoping to knock the stuffing out of their stoic new teammate, but no matter how hard they shot they couldn't rattle the chunky little newcomer. He never complained, didn't swear at them or insult their mothers, even when pucks bounced off his head.

In the Chicago dressing room, Charlie Gardiner found himself being compared to the solemn rookie.

"Hey, that dummy's lookin' better every day. He never yaps at us for not clearing the puck. And you can't fake him out of his jock like some guys we know."

"You're right. He's a lot smarter than our other guy and a lot better-lookin', too. He deserves a start, don't you think?"

"I hear the Major's signed the dummy to a long-term deal. Too bad, but it looks like our regular guy may wind up in the minors."

Gardiner laughed at the jibes, but one day he decided enough was enough. After one scrimmage, he ripped the dummy out of the net, dragged him into the dressing room, and plopped him onto the rubbing table. Gardiner called the trainer over. "Give this poor kid a rubdown, will you? He's falling to pieces out there. Then find some clothes for him, give him a few bucks for a beer and a sandwich, and get him the hell out of here."

McLaughlin's Wife a Designer and a Dancer

M AJOR Fred McLaughlin's wife Irene is credited with designing the Indian head that so prominently adorns the Chicago Blackhawks jersey. Irene is also said to have played a role in the overall design of the Chicago uniforms in the late 1920s and early '30s.

Irene was the widow of and dance partner to Vernon Castle. Together they formed one of the great dancing duos of the era. Her third marriage was to the Chicago coffee baron and her contribution to hockey was color — lots of color. Burly chaps like Lionel Conacher and Johnny Gottselig found themselves wearing striped outfits of red, black, green, and beige. Their stockings were brightened by designs copied from Indian blankets. They may have been the first NHL players to wear light tan gloves, and they were definitely the first to wear gloves with fringed cuffs. Given time, she might have had the Hawks wearing white skates and using multicolored sticks, but her marriage to the Major came unglued, ending in a nasty divorce.

When she sued for divorce, Irene claimed McLaughlin kept their suburban Chicago home so cold that she had to purchase sweaters — colorful ones, no doubt — for her three pet dogs. Later, she complained that the Major had canceled her free pass to the Blackhawks' home games.

On February 16, 1947, the son of the Castle-McLaughlin union made a bit of a mark in the NHL. A major battle erupted during a Chicago-Detroit game at the Stadium. While referee King Clancy was handing out six major penalties, a young man skidded along the ice and leaped at Clancy, fists flying. It was the McLaughlin youth. Clancy knew what punishment to mete out to the players, but he was at a loss when it came to dealing with the son of the former team owner. "What he deserved was a good swift kick in the ass," Clancy growled.

Chicago's First Great Goalie

ALTHOUGH he was born in Edinburgh, Scotland, Charlie Gardiner learned the skills of hockey goaltending on the frosty plains of Winnipeg, Manitoba. Gardiner joined a woeful Chicago team in the late '20s. When he first arrived and witnessed the paucity of talent on the Hawk roster, it's a wonder he didn't turn around and head back to the Manitoba boondocks. And when his team won a mere seven games in his rookie season (1927–28) surely he said to himself, "Charlie my boy, it can't get any worse than this."

But it didn't get any better, either, because the Hawks struggled to another seven victories in his sophomore season.

Gardiner's record after two years was 13 wins, 61 losses, and 10 ties. Even so, Gardiner was regarded as a superb goaltender with incredible skill, and over the next three seasons he proved it, leading the Hawks to three consecutive second-place finishes in the NHL's American Division — and their first appearance in the Stanley Cup finals, in 1931.

When the 1933–34 season rolled around, Gardiner had almost given up his dream of playing on a Stanley Cup winner. The Chicago scorers were pitiful that season, tallying only 88 goals, the poorest offensive production in the NHL. But Gardiner had allowed only 83, ringing up 10 shutouts and compiling a goals-against average of 1.63.

The Blackhawks nosed their way into the playoffs that season and for the next month Gardiner was sensational. Perhaps he had a premonition of darker days ahead. Perhaps he realized this would be his last chance to have his name engraved on Lord Stanley's famous old basin. His backstopping brilliance led the Hawks to a pair of playoff victories — first over the Montreal Canadiens and then the Maroons.

That left two teams in contention for the Cup — the Blackhawks and the Detroit Red Wings. Most hockey people didn't give the Hawks much chance against the powerful Wings, and for good reason: Chicago hadn't won a game in Detroit in three years.

Even Roger Jenkins, one of Gardiner's teammates, had no confidence in the Hawks' prospects. He told Charlie, "You can stand on your head or you can board up the net and the Wings will always find a way to score. If you can find a way to beat them, I'll wheel you around the Loop in a wheelbarrow."

In the opener of the best-of-five series against the Wings, Gardiner turned in an outstanding performance and the Hawks won 2–1. Two nights later, he was just as good in a 4–1 Chicago win. The Red Wings came to life in game three, firing five pucks past a dazed Gardiner en route to a 5–2 thrashing. After that game, teammates Gardiner and Johnny Gottselig — still in their underwear — had words with each other and a scuffle broke out. Team owner Frederic McLaughlin tossed both men in the shower, turned the cold water on, and ordered the two players to "cool off."

Later that night, Gardiner became quite ill and was taken to hospital, where he spent the night. But he insisted on playing in the fourth game at Chicago Stadium and performed superbly. The game was a thriller that remained scoreless after sixty minutes of frantic action. It took more than thirty minutes of overtime before the Hawks' Mush March scored the Stanley Cup–winning goal.

Gardiner's season couldn't have come to a more fitting end. He had lost only one of eight playoff games and compiled a goals-against average of 1.33. He had captured his second Vezina Trophy and been named to the First All-Star Team. And Jenkins made good on his promise, treating Gardiner to a bumpy ride through the Loop in a wheelbarrow.

What Gardiner couldn't have foreseen was that his greatest performance would be his last in the NHL. Two months later, he died of a brain hemorrhage in Winnipeg. He was only 29 years old.

Hit Him Again, Tommy!

HOCKEY fans had never seen anything like it — an NHL manager and a referee tossing punches at each other in front of thousands of screaming fans.

It was the night of March 14, 1933, in Boston. The Bruins and Blackhawks were locked in a 2–2 tie and playing overtime when the bizarre rumpus erupted. In the third minute of the extra period, Boston jumped ahead 3–2 on a goal by Marty Barry. But the game wasn't over. In that era, overtime during the regular season wasn't sudden death: teams played a full ten minutes of extra time.

When Barry scored and the red light flashed, Chicago manager Tommy Gorman was furious. He was certain that the goal judge had flashed the light before the puck had crossed the goal line. When referee Bill Stewart (grandfather of current NHL referee Paul Stewart) skated past the Chicago bench, Gorman reached out and grabbed him by the jersey. He proceeded to fill Stewart's ears with the saltiest language imaginable. When Stewart snarled back, Gorman began throwing lefts and rights at his smaller opponent.

Stewart, who'd had many confrontations with baseball managers in his summer job as a major-league umpire without having to take a single punch, hauled off and socked Gorman once or twice. Gorman retaliated by hauling Stewart's jersey over his head.

Finally, the red-faced referee broke free and skated away from Gorman's flailing fists. He ordered the Chicago manager to the dressing room. When Gorman refused to budge, police moved in and ejected him physically. The Blackhawks, loyal to their boss, left the ice with him. Some of them argued with the police and were threatened with a stint in jail if they didn't behave. In the Chicago dressing room, Gorman told reporters, "Don't blame me, boys. Stewart hit me first. I was simply striking back."

Meanwhile, back on the ice, Stewart pulled out his watch. He gave the Hawks one minute in which to get a lineup back on the ice. When Gorman and the Hawks ignored his ultimatum, he forfeited the match to the Bruins. The two points helped the Bruins into a first-place tie with Detroit atop the NHL's American Division.

It was the first time in NHL history that a coach and his players left the ice with the outcome of a game still in doubt. Referee Stewart refused to discuss the incident, except to say the penalty for such a breach of the rules meant forfeiture of two points and a $1,000 fine.

Ironically, Chicago owner Frederic McLaughlin would hire Stewart four years later to coach his hockey team. The former referee would guide them to a Stanley Cup championship in his first year behind the bench.

Al Melgard Couldn't Skate But He Played for the Hawks

HE played for the Hawks for years and the fans loved him even though he never scored a goal. Al Melgard was the name and organ playing was his game. And man, was he good at it.

A blacksmith's son, he first learned the underlying principles of wind pressure as a child in his father's shop, where he worked the three bellows his father had installed.

Before he'd reached his teens, young Melgard was skilled at pumping to keep pressure up on old church organs. He received his first training from a young female church organist whom he paid twenty-five cents a lesson. By the age of 14 he knew he wanted to be a professional organist someday.

When Chicago Stadium opened in 1929, Melgard was an established musician, hired to play the huge Barton organ that had been installed high against the east wall and suspended from giant steel trusses. A Stadium official bragged that it was the biggest organ in the world, with a keyboard so large "Melgard will need good eyes to see from one end of it to the other."

The spokesman, speaking with a straight face, said, "The organ is so powerful that if it is ever opened full blast the paint will peel from the walls and ceiling, light bulbs in the building will shatter, and the entire arena will shake and wobble on its foundations. The volume is equivalent to twenty-five bands playing all at once."

Flashing a smile, Melgard promised he'd never play it full blast.

He was there to serenade the victors on three Stanley Cup teams. He was there to taunt the game officials with "Three Blind Mice" — until the NHL ordered him to cease and desist. When Doug Bentley scored three goals one night, Melgard struck up "Why Don't We Do This More Often?" And when an opposing coach whined about a goal that was called back, Melgard played "Don't Cry, Joe."

Melgard had access to nine tiers of stops — 883 in all. In front of him were six rows of keys surrounded by a music rack. The organ came with 40,000 pipes of all sizes.

He recorded several albums of music on the famous Stadium organ. Visitors to the arena were just as thrilled to meet Al Melgard as they were to meet any of the Hawks, with the possible exception of Bobby Hull or Stan Mikita.

When the Hawks needed a lift in a game, and Melgard hit those keys that brought forth a "Charge!" the fans responded with a roar that was deafening.

Those were the days, my friend. We thought they'd never end.

Those lyrics would be enough of a cue for Al in days gone by. And the Stadium would jump to his music as he rattled off that song and a dozen others, making everyone in the place feel a whole lot better.

Early in October 1974, Al Melgard took the keys to the giant Barton organ, handed them over to his protégé, Ron Bogda, and retired to Las Vegas.

Earl Seibert's Death Goes Unnoticed

IN May 1990, Earl Seibert, a former hockey superstar, died in the small community of Agawam, Massachusetts, at the age of 78. Seibert was mourned by his family and a number of friends, but his passing went unnoticed by the world of hockey, a world in which he'd once been a towering figure. The NHL sent no representative to his funeral. There were no flowers or calls, not even a card. Seibert was hockey's forgotten man.

Earl Seibert deserved better. He was, after all, a First- or Second-Team All-Star defenseman in ten consecutive NHL seasons. And he was a proud member of the Chicago Blackhawks for almost a decade of his fifteen-year career.

It's been said Seibert preferred to keep a low profile, to step away from the hockey spotlight because he was a bitter, troubled man. His family and friends say he never felt he got the recognition he deserved. He wasn't lauded like others of his era — blueline immortals like Eddie Shore and Dit Clapper. He had soured on the game to the point where he wouldn't even attend his own induction to the Hockey Hall of Fame in 1963. His father Oliver, a famous turn-of-the-century player, had been inducted into the Hall of Fame two years earlier.

Seibert had size, speed, and a gift for anticipation. He was, according to hockey old-timers, the equal of Boston's great star Eddie Shore in almost every way. What set them apart was, perhaps, flair, color, and controversy. Shore played to the crowd and pulled much of the attention away from Seibert and other NHL defenders.

After his playing career, Seibert somehow found himself partnered with Shore as a co-owner of the American Hockey League's Springfield Indians. But Shore's bizarre treatment of staff and players angered and frustrated Seibert. His relationship with the ornery Shore disintegrated and he soon left hockey for good.

As a player he is best remembered for two incidents during his career. On January 28, 1937, the Blackhawks played the Canadiens at the Montreal Forum. The legendary Howie Morenz had returned to the Hab lineup that season, and adoring fans counted on him to rekindle his career, to dazzle them the way he once did.

He made a dash for the puck in the Chicago zone, arriving just as Seibert did. They collided and Morenz went down. Some say he caught his skate blade in a rut, others say Seibert fell on him. The result was a broken leg and Morenz was carried off, never to play again.

Morenz died in hospital a few weeks later. His son, Howie Morenz, Jr., maintains he died of negligence — that the doctors failed to treat a blood clot that traveled to his heart and killed him.

Seibert, until his dying day, felt that he was responsible for the death of Morenz. When a naive young sportswriter asked Seibert if he'd ever played against Morenz, Seibert replied bitterly, "I'm the guy who killed him."

The other incident had a more positive ending. The despondency Seibert felt over Morenz's fate was dispelled — at least temporarily — in the spring of 1938. Playing at right wing for much of the season on a Chicago team guided by a rookie coach (former NHL referee Bill Stewart) — one on which no fewer than eight U.S.–born players performed, a club that won a mere 14 games out of 48 played — Seibert enjoyed a spectacular playoffs, averaging about 55 minutes of every game and helping his team win the Stanley Cup. The Hawks' win over Toronto is remembered as one of the most shocking upsets in Cup history.

The 1938 Champs

CHICAGO'S 1938 Cup-winning team was probably the worst team ever to win the Cup. Their victory was called a fluke, a complete surprise.

How bad were they? Well, consider this:

- They won only 14 of their 48 regular-season games and finished only two points ahead of last-place Detroit.
- The Hawks scored only 97 goals, the weakest offense in the league, while their defense was the NHL's second-most porous, giving up 139 goals.
- Coach Bill Stewart, who'd been an NHL referee and a respected major-league baseball umpire, had never coached hockey in his life. Nor had he been any kind of player.
- Team owner Frederic McLaughlin was so convinced

his team would blow a late-season lead — the Hawks'
last three games were on the road — that he had all the
team's extra equipment shipped back to Chicago. The
Hawks did indeed lose their final three games, but the
rival Red Wings lost two of their last three, allowing
Chicago to back into the playoffs.

- The Hawks had little confidence in themselves. Alex
Levinsky expected an early ouster from the playoffs,
so he emptied his apartment and sent his wife back to
Canada, promising to join her in a few days. He spent
the next month living out of his car.

A Magic Moment
for Alfie Moore

BACKED by the stellar goaltending of Mike Karakas —
the pride of Aurora, Minnesota — the Hawks stunned first the
Montreal Canadiens and then the New York Americans in a pair
of best-of-three series. To their consternation, the Hawks found
themselves facing the Canadian Division–leading Toronto Maple
Leafs, in the Stanley Cup finals.

It looked like their Cinderella ride was about to come to an
end, not only because the Leafs had outpointed Chicago 57–37
during regular-season play, but because Karakas couldn't play!

When he tried to fit his foot into his skates before the opener
at Maple Leaf Gardens, Karakas winced in pain. A broken toe suffered in the previous series had swollen to twice its normal size.
"I can't get my skate on," he announced. "You'll have to find a
substitute."

"But the second-best goalie in our system is playing in
Wichita tonight," moaned manager Bill Tobin. "Maybe the New

York Rangers will lend us their goalie, Dave Kerr. I know he's planning to be at the game tonight."

The Rangers were willing to let Kerr suit up, but Leaf owner Conn Smythe was not.

"Use Kerr? Not on your life," beefed Smythe. "He's too good. But I'll let you use a minor-leaguer — a fellow named Alfie Moore. That is, if you can find him."

A search party consisting of Hawk players Johnny Gottselig and Paul Thompson was sent out. They found Moore in a Toronto tavern, and it was apparent he'd spent most of the afternoon propping up the bar.

Alfie jumped to his feet and called out, "You guys got an extra ticket for the game tonight?" The Chicago players rushed over and shook Alfie's hand. One of them called for Alfie's tab while the other helped him into his topcoat. "Come along with us, Alfie. We're taking you to the game and you don't need a ticket. You'll be standing, not sitting."

When the trio arrived in the Hawk dressing room, coach Bill Stewart called for several cups of hot coffee to be placed in Moore's stall. He suspected his new goalie's reflexes might be slower than usual.

Stewart left the dressing room to find Bill Tobin, his manager, in the corridor, involved in a heated debate with Conn Smythe and his assistant, Frank Selke. Stewart joined the argument, called Selke a liar to his face, and exchanged blows with Smythe. Former Leaf players Harold Cotton, King Clancy, and Joe Primeau emerged from the shadows and grabbed Stewart, who was struggling like a madman and cursing all those around him. Red-faced, he threatened to tear Cotton apart. Finally, Stewart was propelled into the Chicago dressing room. End of round one.

In the famous gondola high over the Gardens ice surface, broadcaster Foster Hewitt commented on Moore's shaky play in the opening minutes of the game. "He appears to be very nervous, as who wouldn't be in his position," observed Hewitt. "And it showed a moment ago when Gordie Drillon scored on the first Toronto shot of the game."

However, if Hewitt and the Leaf fans expected Moore to cave in under a barrage of Leaf shots, they would be disappointed.

Moore pulled himself together after Drillon's blast and managed to put his anxiety aside. He was the picture of composure as he blanked the Leafs the rest of the way. The Hawks won the opener 3–1, with Johnny Gottselig scoring twice for the victors. The Hawks pounded Moore on the back and pumped his hand. As he skated off the ice, the grinning goaltender couldn't resist thumbing his nose at Conn Smythe.

Meanwhile coach Stewart was nursing some bruises he'd picked up during the second intermission. He'd stepped out of the dressing room to chat with a reporter when he spotted Harold Cotton. Hot words were exchanged and suddenly Cotton moved in and landed several punches to Stewart's face and upper body. Stewart slugged back and when bystanders pulled them apart both men were wild with rage. A reporter observed, "It's one of the few games at the Gardens where there were a couple of dandy fights — and the fans didn't see either of them."

Alas, Alfie Moore never got a chance to prove that his splendid performance that night was no fluke. Conn Smythe convinced NHL president Frank Calder that Moore should be declared ineligible for game two — after all, he wasn't Hawk property — and Calder agreed.

Two nights later Paul Goodman, another netminder Bill Stewart had never met, suited up for Chicago and lost, 5–1. "You should have stuck with Alfie," the Leaf fans taunted. Mike Karakas pronounced himself fit for game three and won it on home ice. Then he helped win game four, 4–1, and the Cinderella Hawks had captured the Stanley Cup.

"The big reason for our win," Bill Stewart told reporters, "was Earl Seibert, our great defenseman. He played about 55 minutes in every game and was outstanding in every one of them."

Unfortunately, the underdog Hawks were robbed of a chance to sip champagne from the Stanley Cup after their upset. It seems the Cup was still resting back in Toronto. No one could explain why it was sitting hundreds of miles away, but perhaps no one honestly believed that the Hawks would actually win it. Conventional wisdom must have been that there'd be another game or two in Toronto, so why not leave the Cup there?

The Hawks seethed when they found out they'd have to

celebrate their Cup victory — without the Cup. Veteran Carl Voss was particularly disappointed. He had just completed his final season in the NHL, and while never a big scorer (34 career goals in 261 games with eight different teams), he had popped in the winning goal in the final game against Toronto.

Asked what he thought his contribution to the championship was worth, Alfie Moore said, "How about $150?" The grateful Hawks paid him double that amount and threw in a gold watch, a memento he treasured long after his mediocre career and his one-shot Stanley Cup heroics were history. "I also treasured all the praise I got from the Chicago players, the management, the city, and newspapers nationwide," he said. "As it turned out, I played in only 21 regular-season games in my entire NHL career, none of them with Chicago; and yet, in the only game I played as a Hawk, and thanks to Mike Karakas's sore toe, I got my name engraved on the Stanley Cup. Who'd have believed that would ever happen?"

It's not often a player appears in just one game during a season and gets his name on the Stanley Cup, but two Blackhawks were fortunate enough to do it in 1938: Alfie Moore and Paul Goodman.

The All-American Team

IN January 1937, Major Frederic McLaughlin, the wealthy owner of the Chicago Blackhawks, made a startling announcement. He said he was very unhappy with his team's start (only one win in 12 starts by mid December), so he was going to get rid of all the Canadian players on his club and build a powerful team comprised solely of Americans.

"I'll rename my team the Chicago Yankees," he declared. "By this time next season there'll be only American-born players on the Chicago roster."

He already had four bona fide U.S.–born major-leaguers on his team: goalie Mike Karakas, defenseman Alex Levinsky, and forwards Doc Romnes and Louis Trudel. It's worth noting that all but Karakas had learned their hockey in Canada.

Late in the season, with five games left to play and his Blackhawks destined for a last-place finish in their division, McLaughlin signed five more American-born minor-leaguers to NHL contracts, giving him a total of nine — half the team's roster.

The newcomers were Ernie "Ike" Klingbeil and Paul "Butch" Schaeffer on defense, center Milt Brink, and wingers Bun LaPrairie and Al Suomi. McLaughlin's "pets" received a frosty reception when they joined the club. From the beginning, the remaining Canadians on the Hawk roster treated them as lepers, while players on rival teams taunted them and tried to pound them into the ice.

In their first game, the two rookie defensemen were on the ice for all six Boston goals as the Bruins trounced the revamped Blackhawks 6–2. Manager Art Ross of the Bruins was happy to get the two points, but he protested bitterly to the league that McLaughlin's use of the American-born "amateurs" was farcical.

"Not one of those American greenhorns had a single shot on goal," he griped.

McLaughlin stubbornly kept the new players in the lineup despite widespread criticism. His team won only one of the five remaining games and the rookies looked particularly inept in a 9–4 loss to the New York Americans and a follow-up 6–1 loss to Boston.

While these five players didn't stick with the team, Chicago did add four more American-born players for 1937–38: Carl "Cully" Dahlstrom, Roger Jenkins, Virgil Johnson, and Carl Voss. Despite a poor regular season, this edition of the Blackhawks won the Stanley Cup. If he were alive today, McLaughlin would have no trouble finding enough American-born players to ice a winning combination.

Gottselig Born in Odessa

YOU can stump most of your pals with this bit of hockey trivia. Name the first Russian-born player to play in the NHL.

Some fans with good memories will no doubt mention an obscure Soviet named Victor Nechayev, a native of Siberia and the husband of an American woman who was largely responsible for bringing him to the U.S. in the early '80s. Nechayev had a brief fling with the Los Angeles Kings in 1982–83. He scored one goal in three games before being dispatched to New Haven of the American league. Years later, as a member of the media, he surfaced in Los Angeles, on hand to cover Wayne Gretzky's first game as a King.

But Nechayev is not the name we're looking for. The honor belongs to Johnny Gottselig of the Chicago Blackhawks, who was born in Odessa, Russia, in 1905. Gottselig, whose family moved to Canada when he was just a lad, played in 589 games with the Hawks from 1928–29 to 1944–45. Later he coached the club and worked as a public relations director and broadcaster for the team.

Incidentally, Nechayev wasn't even the second Russian player to play in the NHL. Dave "Sweeney" Schriner, who won back-to-back scoring titles in 1936 and 1937 with the New York Americans, was born in Russia in 1911, even though his birthplace was often listed as Calgary, Alberta.

Chicago Stadium Hosts First NFL Title Game

ON December 18, 1932, the championship of the National Football League was decided in a hockey rink. That week, a raging blizzard swept down from Canada and covered the state of Illinois, leaving football officials in a quandary. As the snow piled up and temperatures plummeted, one bright football man said, "It's impossible to play our title game outdoors. Let's move it indoors — into the Chicago Stadium, home of the Blackhawks."

The Stadium manager readily agreed to the novel idea. Rinkside seats in the Stadium were pushed back several inches while trucks dumped a layer of soil over the floor of the arena. The soil was tramped down and crude line markings were painted over it. By game time the "field" was ready for play and the turnstiles were open. More than 11,000 fans turned out to witness one of the most unusual events in Chicago sports history — a football championship game between the Chicago Bears and the Portsmouth (Ohio) Spartans.

Because the makeshift field was only 80 yards long, every time a team crossed the midpoint it was sent back 20 yards. The star of the Portsmouth team was unable to play because, on the eve of the game, he'd taken a job as basketball coach at Colorado College. Without their best player, Portsmouth failed to score. The Bears scored the game's only touchdown, on a passing play that involved two of the greatest footballers ever: Bronko Nagurski to Red Grange, the "Galloping Ghost." Following their 9–0 defeat, the Spartans pulled up stakes and moved to Detroit, where they changed their name to the Lions.

The strange contest was the first championship game in NFL history, and marked the first and only time an NHL arena was used for an NFL game. It also predated the creation of Arena Football by more than half a century.

Hard Times on
West Madison Street

The Brilliance
of the Bentleys

I N 1950, little Doug Bentley was voted the greatest Blackhawk player of the half century. It was an honor he might well have shared with his brother Max, his equal in every way. But by then, Max Bentley was a Maple Leaf, traded away by manager Bill Tobin early in the 1947–48 season.

A native of Delisle, Saskatchewan, Doug Bentley, at five-foot-eight and 140 pounds, was the smallest of the Chicago athletes named to the half-century team. He joined Luke Appling (baseball), Bronko Nagurski (football), Chick Evans (golf), and Barney Ross (boxing) on a list of Chicago's all-time best. He edged teammate Johnny Gottselig in the hockey category by 86 ballots. At the time, Bentley was the second-highest NHL scorer, with 204 goals. Rocket Richard, with 248, was the leader.

"He was one of the game's marvels," coach Gottselig said of Bentley. "He was the smallest of the great stars of the day, smaller than Howie Morenz but just as good as Morenz. When he first joined the Hawks in 1939 and somebody praised his skills, he said, 'You think I'm good? You should see my brother Max.'

"The Hawks rushed off to sign Max, four years Doug's junior, and a second Bentley became an instant star with the Hawks a year later. There was a third brother, Reg, and we gave him a tryout, too. But Reg failed to last."

Doug led the NHL in goals in 1942–43, with 33, and in 1943–44, with 38. He won the league scoring title in 1943 with 73 points. Max led the league in scoring twice, in 1946 and 1947. Despite the electricity the Bentleys created on ice, their supporting cast was mediocre.

In the mid '40s the Bentley brothers found a perfect linemate in right winger Bill Mosienko, and the Pony Line was formed. Mosienko, cut from the same mold as his linemates at five-foot-eight and 160 pounds, was fast and smart. He played in five All-Star games and scored 258 career goals.

All three members of the Pony Line are in the Hockey Hall of Fame.

Max was shocked when the Hawks broke up the Pony Line by trading him to Toronto. "I loved it in Chicago. I never got over the fact that Doug and I would not play together again. The Leafs tried to get Doug, too, but the Hawks said they wanted ten players for him." Max and Doug did play together again, for the New York Rangers for part of the 1953–54 season.

Old-timers who saw them play claim the Bentleys could skate rings around many of today's players. Rex McLeod, writing in *The Toronto Star*, said Max was "an artist on skates. He bounced around as if the rink was a trampoline. The poets of the day called his perpetual motion style 'dipsy-doodling.'" One called him the "Dipsy-Doodle Dandy from Delisle."

Max was a hypochondriac. He was always moaning about one ailment or another. When he entered the dressing room griping about a headache or a sore knee, his mates would smile. They knew he was ready for a big game. If he entered smiling and chipper, they worried, fearful he would not perform with his usual brilliance.

Shortly after he joined Toronto, Max Bentley told his boss he feared he had cancer — in a vital part of the male anatomy. Team owner Conn Smythe took him aside and told him there was a cure for such an ailment in Scotland and that he would pay the expenses if Max wanted to take the cure.

"What kind of cure?" Max asked

"Well, it's a bit drastic. It means amputation of the afflicted area," was Smythe's reply.

Max said he'd think it over and Smythe never heard him mention the ailment again.

Chicago Fans Hostile to Clancy

AS a referee in the NHL, King Clancy was outstanding. And completely fearless. But Chicago manager Bill Tobin didn't like him much, and complained more than once to NHL president Red Dutton about Clancy's officiating. Dutton's answer was to schedule Clancy for three or four games in a row at the Stadium — just to show Tobin who was boss.

Clancy came through the crowd after a losing effort by the Hawks one night when an irate fan grabbed him by the arm. "Clancy," he said, "one of these nights somebody's going to shoot you dead in here."

King laughed, but later on he began to think he might well be assassinated in the middle of a game. He thought of an incident that took place in the first period of the game that night. He'd leaped up onto the boards and suddenly felt a sharp pain in his backside. He turned to see a lady fan sneering at him and retrieving a long hat pin she'd just plunged into his butt.

Clancy stopped the game and called for the police, demanding they eject the woman. Manager Bill Tobin rushed up and protested. "She's a season ticket holder," he said. "Let her be."

"She's armed and dangerous," Clancy maintained. "Out she goes or you can play this game without a referee." After much argument, the woman was evicted. By then she was a heroine, and she received a round of applause from the fans as she left.

Later that night, carrying his skates and his referee's shirt in a little bag, Clancy found a seat on a crowded streetcar that was taking him back to his hotel. A big fellow sitting next to him struck up a conversation.

"You at the game tonight, bud?"

"Yeah, I was there," Clancy said, guardedly.

"What did you think of that stinkin' referee, that Clancy?"

"Oh, I don't know. What was wrong with him?"

"The guy's a robber. Every time he shows up here he steals a game from us. I'd like to throttle the guy."

Inwardly, Clancy began to laugh. But he kept a poker face when he turned to his new companion.

"Well, I don't know much about hockey. But I can't believe a referee would come here and deliberately try to make Chicago lose."

"Oh, but this Clancy guy does," the man replied. "Every time. Why, the fans on this streetcar would lynch him if they ever got their hands on him."

"My stop coming up," Clancy said, rising to his feet. "Nice to meet you, sir."

He pushed his way through the fans to the exit, breathed a sigh of relief, and walked another ten blocks to his hotel.

Hawks Need Art, Art Kneads Dough

T HAT was the headline in the sports section of a Chicago paper in 1942. Art Wiebe, a solid defenseman who had performed nobly for the Hawks throughout the '30s, was needed back in the Windy City.

But Wiebe was busy in a new career in Vermillion, Alberta. He had opened a small bakery there and spent his days happily putting bread on his customers' tables — and cakes and cookies, too. The aroma from his ovens was much more fragrant than the stale air he'd once inhaled in his former team's dressing room. If he made a small mistake, like dropping a cake on the floor or burning a few cookies, nobody booed, no coach verbally abused him, no red light flashed on to remind him his error had been a costly one.

Still, under his white apron, the lure of hockey was strong in his heart. When the Blackhawks pleaded with him to return, and another Chicago headline read "Hawks Unable to Get Wiebe to Quit His Cookies," he left the bakery business and caught the next train to Chicago, where he could make a lot more dough.

At the end of the 1942–43 season, he went into retirement again. But once more, with a new season under way, the Hawks persuaded him to return. He quit for good in 1944.

Four years later he moved to Edmonton, where he began a new career. In time he became president of the Regent Drilling Company. From 1951 until 1953 he was back in hockey — not as a player, but as coach of the University of Alberta Golden Bears.

Prior to Wiebe's death in 1971, Doug Bentley — a dear friend and teammate from their glory days in Chicago — came to visit. They both suffered from cancer and they knew their days were numbered. Art's wife would remember those few hours as the saddest thing she'd ever seen.

In 1979, Wiebe's grandson, Mark Hemstock, a hockey player himself but never a pro, visited Chicago. Armed with a tattered team photo of the 1941–42 Blackhawks, he convinced a security guard at Chicago Stadium to let him in. He wrote to me and described the few moments he spent there:

It was a memorable experience to walk into that empty 17,000-seat arena. I took a moment to reflect upon the great players of the past and their achievements. Names like Johnny Gottselig, Paul Thompson, Mush March, Mike Karakas, Doug and Max Bentley, and Earl Seibert came to mind. Earl Seibert had been familiar to me since my childhood. I remembered the flood of potato chip bags and candy treats he'd once tossed into the back of our family car when we stopped to see him one summer at his grocery store in Rhode Island. My granddad had been Earl's defense partner for nine years in the NHL.

It was in the Chicago Stadium that the 1938 Stanley Cup was won, but no Cup was presented because it had been left in Toronto. It was here that my grandfather had patrolled the Chicago blue line for 11 seasons, dishing out bone-crunching body checks. I was always so proud of him. Standing in that mammoth Stadium that day was an experience I will never, ever forget.

Sam Was a Survivor

SAM LoPresti was a wartime goalie from Eveleth, Minnesota. He played two seasons with the Blackhawks, after joining the club in 1940. He won 30 games and lost 38.

If Sam is remembered at all it's for a game he played against Boston one night. In 60 minutes he made 80 saves in a game the Bruins won, 3–2. LoPresti saved the match from being a rout. The number of saves he made that night remains an NHL record.

It's one thing to stop pucks; it's another to find yourself facing a German torpedo.

LoPresti joined the navy after his second (and last) NHL season and was aboard the S.S. *Roger B. Taney* in the Atlantic in 1942 when a German U-boat spotted the American ship and blew it apart with two well-aimed torpedoes. Within minutes the *Taney* plunged to the bottom of the ocean.

LoPresti scrambled into a life raft and was later hauled aboard a lifeboat where a couple dozen of his dazed shipmates huddled. The survivors were only a couple of hundred miles from the coast of Africa, but strong winds swept them into the middle of the Atlantic. They had little food, and water was rationed to an ounce a day per man. Sharks circled their small craft and they drifted for a month before a steady rain provided fresh water for drinking. On the forty-second day, LoPresti, who was on watch, spotted land. It was the coast of Brazil.

The survivors were picked up by a Brazilian ship and taken to port, then to hospital. LoPresti had lost 74 pounds during his ordeal. His family had given him up for dead and the navy had reported him missing in action.

When he regained his weight — and his health — LoPresti went back to active duty. He survived the war and returned to Eveleth when it was over.

"Facing 83 shots in a hockey game was child's play compared to facing those torpedoes in the South Atlantic," he once told a reporter.

If LoPresti was proud to be a Blackhawk, he was even prouder to see his son Pete — also a goalie — make the NHL in the '70s. Pete played for six seasons with Minnesota and Edmonton, finishing with a 43–102–20 record.

Smitty Scores First Empty Netter

O N November 11, 1943, the Hawks were leading the Bruins, 5–4, with one minute left to go in a game at Chicago Stadium. Boston manager Art Ross pulled goalie Bert Gardiner from the ice in favor of an extra attacker.

The move backfired when Chicago's Bill Mosienko fed a pass to Clint "Snuffy" Smith, who broke in on the Boston goal. Defenseman Flash Hollett tried to get back to defend the empty net, but he was too late. Smith slipped the puck past him at 19:12 to assure the Hawks of a 6–4 victory, becoming the first NHLer ever to score an empty-net goal.

Smith was a gentlemanly player who served only 24 minutes in penalties during his ten-year career with the Rangers and the Hawks. Imagine playing for a decade and never receiving a major penalty! In three of those seasons he went penalty-free, and in three others he served only two minutes per year. His career high was 6 penalty minutes in his final season, 1946–47.

Smith is one of only seven Chicago players — and the least famous of them — to average more than a point per game. The others are Stan Mikita, Bobby Hull, Denis Savard, Steve Larmer, Jeremy Roenick, and Max Bentley. Smith played in 215 games as a Blackhawk and compiled 217 points.

Bodnar's Two Remarkable Records

FORMER Blackhawk Gus Bodnar never gets tired of discussing two impressive NHL records — fastest goal by a rookie and the league's fastest three assists. That's because he owns both of them.

Now 77, Bodnar has waited a long time for someone to snap his record for the fastest goal by a player in his first NHL game — 15 seconds. He set that mark as a Maple Leaf in the opening game of the 1943–44 season. Two other players have threatened Bodnar's mark. Buffalo's Danny Gare scored 18 seconds from the start of his first game in 1974, and another Sabre, Alexander Mogilny, scored after 20 seconds of play in his 1989 debut.

Bodnar claimed rookie-of-the-year honors in 1944 and won two Stanley Cups as a Leaf, but he was dealt to Chicago in 1947. It was there that he would set the record that's even less likely to be broken. Bodnar's passes set up Bill Mosienko for three goals in the span of just 21 seconds.

Mosienko's hat trick came in New York on March 23, 1952, in the final game of the 1951–52 season. In the Ranger net was an obscure, green-as-grass rookie from Renfrew, Ontario, named Lorne Anderson. Anderson would play only three games in the NHL and this would be his last. In his brief career he gave up 18 goals and bowed out with a 6.00 goals-against average.

"Mosienko was a great little player," Bodnar recalls. "When I took the face-off for the first of his three goals he was already in flight because he liked to circle and get a running start. I threw the puck over and he went around the defenseman on his side and scored. A few seconds later, I won the draw again, threw the puck over to Mosey and he scored again.

"The Rangers made a change then and put a better face-off man up against me. This time when I won the draw I sent the puck over to George Gee on the left side. He threw a long pass to Mosey and bingo! The puck was in the net. We kind of laughed because our line had scored three goals and two of us on the line hadn't done a bit of skating. Mosey had taken care of everything."

Culture Shock in Chicago for Bodnar

BEFORE he was traded to Chicago on November 2, 1947, Bodnar played on two Stanley Cup–winning teams in Toronto. Upon his arrival in the Windy City, he noticed a shocking difference in his new team's approach to the game.

"With the Leafs it was all business. We were told to wear jackets and ties and behave ourselves, or else. Conn Smythe and Hap Day wouldn't have it any other way. We were told to attend charity functions and hockey banquets for kids and we'd darn well better show up and sign every autograph book held out to us or we'd hear about it.

"What a difference in Chicago! Talk about a relaxed attitude. We could wear T-shirts or anything else we chose to wear. Every day there were card games under way — like gin rummy. And if the coach ordered us on the ice for a practice the players would tell him to hold on a minute, they'd put their uniforms on once the card game was over. It was unbelievable. No wonder we didn't win too many hockey games."

Gadsby a Survivor

BILL Gadsby, the Hall of Fame defenseman, was involved in a lot of rough hockey games in his life and has more than 500 stitches in his face and on his body to prove it.

But no hockey game, no matter how nasty, ever terrified him or caused him to worry about survival as much as an experience he went through as a 12-year-old boy.

He was with his mother on a three-month trip from Calgary to England to visit relatives when war broke out in 1939. Despite his youth, Bill volunteered to help build air raid shelters and remembers being terrified when the first German bombers roared overhead, en route to Liverpool.

Meanwhile, his mother spent four frantic weeks trying to book passage back home and felt extremely fortunate when she was able to reserve two tickets on the *Athenia*, the last Canada-bound liner to leave the Southampton docks.

The Gadsbys were asleep when a Nazi torpedo slammed into the ship, ripping it apart.

"We were knocked right out of our berths by the explosion," Gadsby recalls. "My mother rushed me up to one of the lifeboats where men and women were going crazy with panic. I saw some pretty horrible sights. I remember how calm my mother was through it all when everyone else appeared to be going mad.

"Our lifeboat was jammed with about fifty passengers. The water was rough and cold and it was pitch dark. I don't think we had anything to eat but I remember we had tea to drink. The English always have tea."

Within a few hours the survivors were picked up by another

ship and returned to Southampton. Days later, aboard the *Mauretania*, the Gadsbys finally arrived home via New York.

"My dad was glad to see us. He had heard all about the *Athenia* going down, but it was days before a list of survivors was made public. For quite a while he had no idea what had happened to us."

Back in Calgary, his brush with death behind him, Gadsby developed into quite a hockey player.

As a teenager, he was scouted for Chicago by Tiny Thompson. He committed to Chicago at 19, signed by Bill Tobin, who later became the Hawks' president. He spent two years in Junior hockey at Edmonton and, after a mere 12 games with Kansas City, was brought up to the Hawks for what remained of the 1946–47 season.

"I was a left winger at Kansas City," he says, "but when I got called up to Chicago the club had a lot of injuries so they put me on defense. I never played another game up front.

"I made a lot of mistakes when I was first in the league. Ran around a lot on the ice. Then Charlie Conacher took over from Johnny Gottselig as coach and he straightened me out. Ebbie Goodfellow, who succeeded Conacher, showed me the art of taking a man out, forcing an opponent to go wide, pushing guys into the corners, that sort of thing. He was a great help to me."

Gadsby played twenty years in the NHL, eight and a half of them with Chicago. One season, early in his career, he contracted polio but was able to beat the disease that crippled thousands in the era before Dr. Salk's vaccine.

Gadsby had more than his share of injuries, including a broken leg, a shoulder separation that came apart two or three times, and a nose that was ripped open by a hockey stick.

"That nose injury hurt the most," he recalls. "They didn't freeze it and I'll wager my fingerprints are still on that table where they placed me to stitch me up."

Gadsby knew his days as a Blackhawk might be numbered when Tommy Ivan was brought in from Detroit to run the club. The season before, during a game against the Red Wings, Gadsby had hot words with Ivan after a scrap near the Detroit bench.

47

"I called him every name in the book," he laughs. "Now he comes to Chicago as my new boss. I asked my wife Edna, 'You think he'll remember all those names I called him that night in Detroit?' She said, 'I would if I were him.'

"I'm not saying that's why he traded me, I mean, I did hold out for more money that fall and I failed to report for training camp. Maybe he just had enough of me. Anyway, it wasn't long before I found myself playing for the Rangers."

Often, when Bill Gadsby's name surfaces, the conversation centers on his brief coaching career rather than on his lengthy playing career. After retiring as a Detroit Red Wing in 1966, he was asked to come back in 1969 and coach the Wings. He got off to a grand start, coaching his club to two straight victories. Then, inexplicably, he was fired by Detroit owner Bruce Norris. Nobody has ever figured out exactly why. How often does a coach with a perfect record get the gate? But Norris was a strange bird with a drinking problem and not all of his decisions made a great deal of sense.

Conacher Assaults Ref and Writer

BIG Charlie Conacher enjoyed phenomenal success on the ice as a player. As a coach, it was a different story. In close to three years behind the Chicago bench — from mid 1947–48 through 1949–50 — his teams never made the playoffs, finishing last in two of the seasons and second-last in the other.

Little wonder, then, that Conacher was seething with frustration and anger during a game at the Detroit Olympia on February 8, 1950. His Hawks were being pummeled by Howe, Lindsay, Abel, and Company — 9–2 was the final score — and one of his best players was crumpled on the ice, looking as if he might never see the sun rise in the morning.

"Doug Bentley was charged by the Wings' George Gee and lay there, his legs quivering. I thought he was dead," Conacher told reporters afterward. "And that bleepin' referee, Bill Chadwick, didn't even call a penalty. He always favors the front-runners, anyway. To hell with the guys on the bottom.

"Then he wouldn't come to the bench to talk to me. I told one of my players to tell him the game wouldn't start again until he did. Well, he came over and told me he didn't see it and neither did the linesmen. Hell, it happened in front of everybody and they didn't see it."

Witnesses claim Conacher reached out and grabbed Chadwick by his jersey, forcing the referee to wrestle his way into the clear. "If Conacher had put his big mitts around Chadwick's neck, it might have been curtains," one bystander said.

In the Chicago dressing room after the game, the irate coach assaulted another of his enemies, this time a reporter for a Detroit paper.

"I have no use whatsoever for Lew Walter of the Detroit *Times*," Conacher said by way of explanation. "The bleeper called me a bleepety-bleep and I don't have to take that from anyone."

Walter had recently written that a new coach for Chicago might not be a bad idea.

"How many times did you hit him?" Conacher was asked by a newspaperman who wisely kept his distance.

"It was only necessary for me to hit him once," replied Charlie. In his playing days, one blow was often more than enough to do away with an enemy.

Walter's account was quite different. "I was talking things over with Charlie when he blew up and criticized some of the stories I'd written about Chicago in the past couple of seasons. The next thing I knew I was on the floor, with Conacher on top of me and his hands around my throat. We wrestled around for a minute or two and then Charlie got up and ordered me out of the room. I stayed right there until Doug Bentley, a friend of mine, came over and suggested it would be better if I left. So I did."

The following day, Walter filed assault-and-battery charges against Conacher. When Conacher called to apologize, Walter withdrew the charges.

Conacher resigned as Chicago coach at the end of the season, saying, "I've had it with hockey. Three years of this kind of life is more than enough for anyone."

Norris and Wirtz
Take Charge

Old Man Roberts
Gets the Call

THERE'S a famous story about New York Ranger coach Lester Patrick taking over in goal during a Stanley Cup game in Montreal in 1928. Patrick, then 44, substituted for injured netminder Lorne Chabot and stymied the Maroons, stopping all but one shot until his team won the match in overtime.

Less publicized, but almost as impressive, was the goaltending of Moe Roberts, a Blackhawk trainer who got the call one night during the 1951–52 season. On November 24, just a couple of weeks short of his 46th birthday, Roberts was asked to don the pads when regular goalie Harry Lumley was injured and forced to leave a game against first-place Detroit. Roberts, a native of Waterbury, Connecticut, had retired from a minor-league goaltending career a decade earlier, although he'd returned briefly in 1945–46 with the Washington Lions of the Eastern league.

Roberts huffed and puffed his way through twenty minutes of action and shut out the high-scoring visitors. Chicago won the match 6–2. Then it was back to his training duties for Roberts, who for years could boast, "I was the oldest player ever to suit up for a game in the NHL."

In 1980–81, Gordie Howe — at age 52 — played in all 80 games for the Hartford Whalers, rendering Roberts's feat insignificant. And Leaf netminder Johnny Bower, who played his last game in December 1969, never divulged his age, and was thought by many to be well into his late forties when he retired. Officially, he was a month past his 45th birthday.

Still, Roberts was delighted to go out a winner — and with one-third of a shutout.

Mosienko Sinks
Three Fastest

WAYNE Gretzky had 50 hat tricks in his illustrious career, but he never scored three goals in 21 seconds. That remarkable record, which has stood for nearly half a century, is held by Bill Mosienko, who toiled for the Blackhawks from 1941–42 until 1954–55.

Mosienko was a winner on a team that seldom strayed out of last place. He played in five All-Star games and won the Lady Byng Trophy in 1945. But, during his 14-year career, Chicago finished last or second-last in the NHL standings ten times!

Of Mosienko's 258 career goals, three would always be close to his heart and easily recalled, not only by him but by everybody who knew him.

On March 23, 1952, the Blackhawks journeyed to New York to close out their regular season against the Rangers. The Hawks had won only 16 games that season and were destined to finish in last place for the third year in a row. If they lost their match at Madison Square Garden, Chicago would finish a distant 20 points behind the fifth-place Rangers.

"We've had another disastrous season," Bill Mosienko reminded his teammates before the game. "Let's try hard to win our final game."

Earlier in the season, Mosienko had mentioned to a teammate, "You know, it doesn't look like I'll ever get to play on a Stanley Cup winner. But I'd sure like to do something in hockey that I'll be remembered for."

He was to get his wish — in spades.

Fewer than 2,500 fans would witness Mosienko's shining moment. The Garden was almost deserted, and no wonder. Who wanted to pay good money to see a meaningless game between the NHL's doormats?

What's more, popular Ranger goalie Chuck Rayner had been

injured a few days earlier. In his place was a rookie, 20-year-old Lorne Anderson.

A few years ago, in Winnipeg, I encountered Bill Mosienko and asked him what he remembered of that game.

"How could I ever forget it?" he said, his eyes glistening. "I scored three goals in record time and I almost scored a fourth. Gus Bodnar was my centerman, you know, and he set a record, too — for the three fastest assists. We won the game 7–6 after trailing 6–2. But let me tell you about my goals.

"When Gus sent me the puck off the face-off I was already in motion. I cut around the opposing winger and went around defenseman Hy Buller, who was playing on a bad ankle, and cut in on goal. Now this kid Anderson had already beat me three times and I thought to myself, he's not going to touch this one. I slid the puck along the ice on his right side and the light went on. Never thought much about it, except it was my 29th goal of the year. But for some reason I hauled the puck out of the net to keep it as a souvenir. Remember, in those days a 30-goal season was a tremendous feat. I gave the puck to our coach, Ebbie Goodfellow, and told him to keep it for me.

"So now we go back for the face-off and Bodnar gets the puck over to me again. I whip around my winger and whip around the same defenseman and cut in on goal again. And I put the puck in the net exactly the same way as I did it before. I scrambled into the net to dig the puck out, thinking, heck, I don't want the 29th goal puck, I want the 30th. And I gave that puck to Ebbie Goodfellow.

"Now we come back to center ice and face off again. This time Bodnar sends the puck over to our left winger, George Gee, and he raced up with it. He threw it over to me — a perfect pass — and I sailed around Buller, the same defenseman I'd just beaten twice, and I cut in on goal for a third time. But this time I'm thinking this Anderson kid is no dummy; he's going to figure me for the same shot. Only this time I pulled him out and threw it high into the corner of the net. I'd scored three times — just like that.

"That's when Jimmy Peters, my teammate, yelled at me from the bench, 'Mosie, Mosie, grab that puck. It's a record!'

"Heck, I didn't know anything about a record. But I grabbed

the puck and took it to Ebbie. I said, 'Ebbie, hold on to this for me.' That's how Ebbie managed to collect all three pucks and they took a photo of me holding them up after the game.

"When I think back to those days and how I wanted to leave some sort of a mark in hockey, I never dreamed it would be by scoring the three fastest goals. It seems everybody remembers me for that. Hardly a day goes by without somebody wanting me to talk about it. And I'm sorry I helped end the career of the kid goalie, Anderson. He never played another game."

"Mosie always displayed class and dignity on and off the ice," said Jack Fitzsimmons, secretary of the Blackhawks alumni association. "I dare anyone to find one disparaging word ever written or said about him during his career."

Rollins a Member of an Exclusive Club

ONLY two NHL goalies have ever captured the Vezina Trophy, the Hart, and the Stanley Cup. Jacques Plante was one, and Al Rollins of the Chicago Blackhawks was the other.

What made Rollins's Hart Trophy win in 1954 so astonishing is that he did it with a last-place team. The lackluster Hawks won only 12 games all season, but it's possible they might not have won any games without Rollins's superb goaltending. League moguls were so impressed they named Elwin Ira (Al) Rollins the NHL's most valuable player. He was amazed, if not downright flabbergasted, at the unexpected recognition.

"I couldn't believe it," Rollins would say. "How often does a goalie with a last place club, one that gave up 242 goals, receive such an honor? Heck, my goals-against average that season was 3.23."

By comparison, when Plante won the Hart a few years later, in 1962, his Canadiens had sailed through a season with 42 wins and 98 points, tops in the NHL in both categories. Plante had 4 shutouts and a goals-against average of 2.37.

Rollins is one of only five goalies ever to win the Hart Trophy. The others were Plante, Roy Worters (1929), Chuck Rayner (1950), and Dominik Hasek (1997 and '98).

Rollins also earned his Vezina Trophy the hard way. Called up to the Leafs in 1950, he shared the goaltending duties with aging Turk Broda. The lanky rookie from Vanguard, Saskatchewan, played in 40 of Toronto's 70 games and clinched the Vezina by a single goal over Detroit's Terry Sawchuk — only after recording shutouts in two of his final three games. That season, Rollins was runner-up to Sawchuk for the Calder Trophy as top freshman.

There was more glory to follow that spring. Rollins played the final three games of the 1951 Toronto–Montreal Stanley Cup final series. Do you recall, or have you read about that one — the series in which all the games went into overtime? Surely you know of Bill Barilko's dramatic overtime marker against Gerry McNeil that ended game five and brought the Cup to Toronto! Barilko was killed in a plane crash a few months later.

Rollins had the Toronto goaltending job all to himself the following season, then Conn Smythe dealt him to Chicago, along with Cal Gardner, Gus Mortson, and Ray Hannigan, for veteran goaltender Harry Lumley. His second season as a Blackhawk, 1953–54, saw Rollins win the Hart Trophy.

Although he was the league's MVP, the All-Star voters overlooked Rollins. Instead, they named Toronto's Harry Lumley to the First Team and Sawchuk to the Second. They'd also snubbed him in his Vezina-winning season of 1951.

Rollins remained a Blackhawk until 1957, when another trade — a blockbuster with Detroit — brought Glenn Hall into the fold.

A Dynamite Deal
with Detroit . . .

THE Detroit Red Wings were an NHL powerhouse in the 1950s. They won Stanley Cups in 1950, '52, '54, and '55 before the Montreal Canadiens took over and captured the Cup for a record five straight seasons.

After a couple of seasons playing second fiddle to the Habs, Jack Adams — the crusty Red Wings manager — decided to make some changes, starting with two players who were in his doghouse. Veteran left winger Ted Lindsay had had the audacity to help establish a Players Association, an act that infuriated Adams. Meanwhile, young goaltender Glenn Hall had sassed him back one day in the Red Wing dressing room. Adams would make sure Lindsay and Hall paid a stiff price for daring to question his leadership: he would ship the disgruntled pair off to Chicago, last-place finishers for the past four years.

As far as Adams was concerned, the duo was expendable. Hall wasn't needed, despite his bright future, because Terry Sawchuk, the best goalie in hockey, was still in his prime and back in the Detroit fold after a two-year exile to Boston. And though Lindsay had been the league's second-highest scorer in 1957, he was simply getting too big for his britches.

The Blackhawks offered Johnny Wilson, Forbes Kennedy, Hank Bassen, and William Preston. Adams jumped at the deal.

Both Lindsay and Hall would have an immediate impact in the Windy City. Terrible Ted finished third in team scoring behind Ed Litzenberger and Bobby Hull, while Hall played in all 70 games and drew rave reviews for his play. Over the next decade he would become one of the greatest netminders in NHL history.

To this day, Lindsay has no regrets about being traded to Chicago.

"I was traded because I was behind the formation of the

Players Association and the trade happened right after I had my best year as a Red Wing. The players needed an association. We needed a voice. We weren't interested in running hockey. We weren't asking for much. But back then the six-team league was a dictatorship. The owners would say 'Jump' and we'd all start jumping.

"In Detroit, Jack Adams was praying I'd have a bad season so he could hang me out. He hadn't spoken to me the last three years I was there. But I didn't play hockey for Adams, I played hockey because I loved it.

"As for Glenn Hall, I think he was thrown into the deal because he was a Ted Lindsay fan. For the next fifteen years, Hall was the best in the league.

"Unfortunately, I played only one good season as a Blackhawk. My first year there I saw Bobby Hull break in, and then Stan Mikita came along. Both great players. But I found I was existing in Chicago — not really living. So after my third season I called it quits."

. . . And a Dud

ON November 2, 1947, Chicago traded ace centerman Max Bentley, the game's most famous hypochondriac, along with little-known Cy Thomas, to the Toronto Maple Leafs for Gus Bodnar, Bud Poile, and Gaye Stewart — the Leafs' famous Flying Forts Line — along with defensemen Bob Goldham and Ernie Dickens.

Even though the newcomers helped the Hawks at both ends of the rink, Bentley was a puck magician, a superstar, one of the greatest players in NHL history. He was a major factor in the Leafs' three Stanley Cups over the next four seasons. Hawk fans mourned the loss of Bentley, who became a Hall of Famer.

Even Chicago manager Bill Tobin would one day tell Bentley, "Trading you was the biggest mistake I ever made."

"Chief" Saskamoose Was the First Treaty Indian in the NHL

H IS brief NHL career with the Blackhawks lasted only 11 games, in which he scored no goals or points. It was during the 1953–54 season, another of several dismal campaigns for the moribund Hawks, and an inopportune time perhaps for Fred Saskamoose, a Canadian Indian from Saskatchewan's Sandy Lake Reserve, to be called to hockey's major league.

He had signed with the Hawks at age 16 for a $100 bonus — big money for an "Indian from the bush," as he often referred to himself. Four years later, he was finishing his Junior A career in Moose Jaw, Saskatchewan. He centered a line with a Chinese player on one wing and a black player on the other. All three suffered the slings and arrows of ignorant fans around the league who delighted in hurling insults and racial epithets at the trio. By then, Saskamoose was Regina's team captain and top player, scoring 31 goals in 34 games.

The Hawks, destined for another last-place finish, ordered Saskamoose to join them in Toronto for a game against the Leafs. When he stepped off the train he couldn't believe the size of the city. When he checked into the Royal York Hotel across the street from the railway station he told the clerk, "This is the biggest building I've ever seen."

Interviewed by reporters prior to his first game, Saskamoose was asked to speak in Cree — and he did. One scribe, no doubt a fan of Western movies, raised his hand and said, "How!" Saskamoose shot back, "Howe. Gordie Howe." Everybody laughed.

Pete Conacher, the Hawks' leading scorer that season with 19 goals, remembers Saskamoose as "an energetic skater." He told writer Tom Hawthorn the rookie was "nervous, unsure of himself, just like we all were when we were first called up. And we weren't able to help him much because we were a last-place team. I remember that he wasn't very big, about five-foot-eight and 160 pounds, and the sweater he wore almost came down to his knees."

His mates promptly tagged Saskamoose with the nickname "Chief," and when he warmed up prior to his first game at Chicago Stadium the organist played "Indian Love Call." It seemed fitting that the first treaty Indian to play in the NHL was wearing a jersey with a huge Indian head on the front.

Saskamoose finished the season with the Blackhawks and tried desperately to score a goal. He came close a few times but never basked in the red light's glow.

At the end of the season, on his way back to the Sandy Lake Reserve, he stopped in Regina and bought a 1954 Dodge for $3,900. There were no roads on the reserve, and no one there owned a car. So when word spread that Fred Saskamoose, the famous hockey hero, was driving a car down the rutted trail to his family's log home, crowds gathered to gawk and cheer. They shook his hand, pounded his back, and sought his autograph.

In the fall it was time for hockey again. Fred attended training camp, but the Hawks had acquired some new players and he failed to impress. He was sent to Chicoutimi, in far-off Quebec. Later he played in New Westminster and Calgary. Along the way he acquired two more nicknames — Chief Running Deer and Chief Thunderstick. He never scored many goals, only a handful every season, until 1957–58, when he tallied 26 times for the Kamloops (British Columbia) Chiefs.

One day his wife delivered an ultimatum. "It's me or hockey," she said bluntly. Saskamoose wisely gave up the game.

Today, at 67, he lives not far from the slough on which he skated as a kid. Around Sandy Lake he remains a hero to his friends and neighbors — and especially to his thirty-five grandchildren and four great grandchildren.

Asked about his brief NHL stint, he mentions one lingering regret. "If I could have scored just one goal in the NHL, I'd be happier. I came so close, but I didn't score. If I had, then I'd have a puck to keep, one I could show to everybody."

Tod Sloan Retired Happy

ALOYSIUS Martin Sloan, better known as "Tod" or "Slinker" Sloan, was a star player for the Toronto Maple Leafs from 1950–51 until 1957–58. He was banished to the Blackhawks in June 1958 for daring to support the idea of a Players Association.

This tough, resilient forward with the quick, shifty moves was only one of several "agitators" who were punished with one-way tickets to Chicago, then known as hockey's Siberia. And the Blackhawks, ever desperate for help, were happy to provide a home for players branded as malcontents and troublemakers by other league moguls.

Toronto owner Conn Smythe once said of the strong-willed Sloan — a league All-Star in 1956 after a 37-goal season — "Tod's his own boss. The best way to handle him is to leave him alone." Of course that was so much Smythe malarkey. If you wore a Leaf jersey in those days, you had only one boss: Conn Smythe. And he seldom left any of his players alone — he even banished one player to the minors for daring to get married in midseason.

Even though the Leafs had finished at the bottom of the standings in 1957–58 and could use some fresh legs, Sloan was sent packing — not for players, but for cash, and not a lot of it, either.

It wasn't the first time Smythe had dispatched a union supporter to the Blackhawks. In August 1957 he sold defenseman Jim Thomson to Chicago. Thomson retired from hockey before Sloan's arrival in the Windy City, but Ted Lindsay, a former

Detroit great exiled to Illinois after he helped form the union, was there to greet the former Leaf. They played on a line together, with Ed Litzenberger at right wing. It was called the Pappy Line because all three were beginning to show their age.

On October 11, the Blackhawks opened the 1958–59 season in Toronto at Maple Leaf Gardens. Leaf coach Billy Reay, beginning his second season, had added goaltender Johnny Bower, defenseman Allan Stanley, and former Hab Bert Olmstead to his lineup.

After two periods, the Leafs were leading 1–0. During the intermission, coach Reay was interviewed on TV by *Hockey Night in Canada*'s Scott Young. Reay told Young he'd have something more to say about his team after the game — if the Leafs prevailed.

Reay never made it back to the studio. Tod Sloan scored the tying and winning goals as Chicago fought back for a 3–1 victory. Young, who was also a columnist for *The Globe and Mail*, would write: "Defeat had an extra sourness, because some of the biggest cheers of the night had an undertone of jeering. The cheers had been for Tod Sloan and his goals, and for Chicago. The jeers were for the Leafs. After paying for Sloan's education in both school and hockey since age 15, Smythe had sold him to Chicago, the last of the old NHL Players Association activists to be cleaned out."

The Slinker had extracted a good measure of revenge in his first game back at Maple Leaf Gardens. He was beaming as he skated out to be recognized as the first star of the evening's performance. Some fans taunted Stafford Smythe, Conn's son: "Hey, Staff, how'd you like to buy Sloan back?"

Sloan was just as slippery when the clubs met the next night at Chicago Stadium. He scored two more goals in a 5–2 Blackhawk romp.

Sloan proved to be a valuable acquisition for the Blackhawks. Not only did he finish the 1958–59 season with 27 goals and 62 points — four points short of his career high — he helped lead his new team to third place in the NHL standings, a height they hadn't reached since the 1945–46 season. In fact, the Hawks had finished dead last nine times during the twelve-year interval.

The Old Redhead's
Last Game

─────────

IT was the spring of 1959 and the Chicago Blackhawks, after wallowing in the NHL basement — or close to it — for most of the decade, found themselves in the Stanley Cup playoffs.

Their first-round opponents, the Montreal Canadiens, were the class of the league, en route to their fourth consecutive Cup triumph and heavy favorites to eliminate the Hawks. Montreal's 91 points put them 22 ahead of Chicago, who'd lost five of their final six regular-season games, including an 8–4 drubbing at the Forum.

Still, the Hawks felt they had a chance to engineer a major upset in the postseason. After losing their first two playoff games at the Forum, the Hawks rebounded to square the series with a pair of wins on home ice. When Montreal captured game five, they led the series three games to two.

Chicago coach Rudy Pilous personally asked referee-in-chief Carl Voss to assign veteran ref Red Storey to handle the whistle-tooting chores in game six. If Storey had known what perils were waiting for him at Chicago Stadium he might have declined with thanks.

From the moment the teams skated out for the opening whistle the arena was in an uproar. With close to 20,000 fans screaming, stamping their feet, and guzzling beer, and with frequent blasts from the cacophonous Barton pipe organ stirring emotions, nothing short of victory was going to satisfy the rabid Hawk supporters in the crowd that night.

Storey and his two linesmen successfully controlled the game through two periods, although Storey recalls stopping by the boards at one point and seeing a fan pull his coat back to reveal a gun. "Storey, I'm going to blow your brains out," the spectator snarled. Two cops rushed in and led the man away.

─────────

With seven minutes to play in the third period, the score was tied 3–3. Big Eddie Litzenberger, a former Hab who was Chicago's leading scorer, started out of his own zone when he stepped on the blade of a Montreal player's stick. Litz sprawled on the ice and the crowd was incensed when Storey failed to call a penalty. They were doubly incensed when Dickie Moore scored for Montreal a few seconds later, putting the Habs in front 4–3. But Ted Lindsay beat Jacques Plante for a goal to tie the score and the fans settled back, catching their breath and letting their anger cool.

With less than two minutes to play, left winger Bobby Hull flew down the ice and was flattened at the Montreal blue line by a thunderous hip check from Junior Langlois. Hull sprawled on his backside à la Litzenberger, but again referee Storey saw no crime and called no penalty. While the fans assaulted Storey with their verbal venom, Montreal's Claude Provost stole the puck and raced in to score. Montreal 5, Chicago 4.

Even though there was still time to score — more than a minute remained on the clock — the Hawks, their fans, everyone in the Stadium knew the curtain had come down with a thud on another season.

There would be no Stanley Cup for Chicago, no parade, no party, and all because of the robber Red Storey, who stood stoically at center ice, waiting to resume play.

Debris filled the air. Bottles, cans, coins, programs, anything that could be pried loose and hurled at Storey came crashing down on the ice until the entire surface was almost covered with garbage.

Suddenly, Storey turned to face a fan who had jumped over the boards. The man skidded across the ice and hurled a cupful of beer squarely in the referee's face.

Storey was furious. "I drew back my fist, ready to plow the guy. Then I heard Doug Harvey, Montreal's top defenseman, shout at me. 'Don't hit him, Red! You can't hit a fan.' So I hesitated. But Harvey had no such qualms. He belted the guy right in the puss. Pow! Then Harvey belted him again and the fan staggered off, barely able to crawl back over the boards. Then Harvey shouts, 'Look out!' Another guy had jumped the fence and raced over. He tried to leap on my back. When he jumped on me I kind of dipped and caught him with my shoulder and flipped him in the air. When he was up there, Harvey clubbed him with his stick and cut him for about eighteen stitches. That was enough. The guy skidded along the ice, bleeding profusely, looking like he'd just come out of a slaughterhouse."

The flow of blood — and Harvey's heavy stick — discouraged other would-be assassins from coming out in an effort to make a corpse of Storey. Stadium workers sprang into action and began to scrape the litter from the ice.

Storey, meanwhile, considered forfeiting the game to Montreal and wondered how the fans would react to that news. They'd probably burn the building down, he thought. He wanted to discuss the situation with Clarence Campbell, the league president, who was sitting behind the Chicago bench. But Campbell refused to make eye contact with Storey and the message was clear: You got yourself into this, Mr. Storey. Now get yourself out of it.

Finally the ice was cleaned and play resumed. But the Hawks failed to score and Montreal advanced to the finals and, eventually, to another Stanley Cup.

After the game, the Hawks' Danny Lewicki handed Storey his hockey stick. "You might need this to get out of this place alive," he warned.

Storey used the stick to hold back irate fans who wanted to tear him apart as he made his way to the officials' room. In the corridor, he encountered Terrible Ted Lindsay, who brandished a stick and snarled at him, "I'm going to take your head off." Storey waved Lewicki's stick in Lindsay's face and snarled back, "Make it fast, Ted, because I may just carve you in two."

Suddenly Blackhawks boss Jim Norris was between them. He shoved Lindsay into the Hawks' dressing room and told Storey, "Red, you don't have to take any crap from my players or anyone else in my arena."

After a shower, Storey confronted Clarence Campbell. "Why didn't you come down and meet with me when you could see a riot was about to happen?"

"Because I feared for my life," Campbell replied. "I was afraid I wouldn't get out of there alive."

Storey recalls that it was an honest remark, even though it was *his* life, not Campbell's, that was at stake. Storey and his mates needed a police escort to get safely back to their hotel.

Later, when they met at a nearby tavern for a few beers, the bartender hollered, "Hey, Storey, there was a guy in here a few minutes ago with a gun. Said he was going to shoot you." The gunman never came back but the fallout from Storey's night's work was far from over — even after he'd left town, bound for Boston and his next playoff assignment.

In Boston, Red discovered that Campbell had accused him of choking during the final game at the Stadium. It was in all the papers: Campbell Says Storey Choked. Campbell was quoted in the Ottawa *Journal* as saying that Storey had missed the tripping penalties on Hull and Litzenberger, and that he'd almost precipitated a riot by not putting the puck in play after Montreal's final goal. The league president tried to claim his remarks had been taken out of context, but Storey didn't buy it. He resigned on the spot. He didn't see or speak to Clarence Campbell for the next five years and he never saw Voss — "the weakest man I've ever known" — ever again.

Watson Shocked at Blackhawks' Approach

"**H**OW did you enjoy playing for Chicago?" I ask Hall of Famer Harry Watson, just turned 75. We're at our monthly meeting of the NHL Old-Timers in Markham, Ontario, and sitting next to Harry is a former Chicago teammate, Gus Bodnar. Across the table from us is former Leaf star Wally Stanowski.

"It wasn't at all what I thought it would be," he replies. "After playing in Detroit and Toronto, I was shocked at what went on in Chicago. There was no organization at all. You'd play a Wednesday-night game and the next game would be three days later on Saturday. You wouldn't see any of the guys. They'd scatter all over. There'd be no practice. The whole situation seemed to be out of control most of the time.

"I had a little run-in with manager Tommy Ivan when I was there. And the coach, Frank Eddolls, got involved. We played a Wednesday-night game and our next game was in Toronto on Saturday, where my home was. Since we didn't practice often, I asked Eddolls for permission to go home after the game and see my family for a couple of days. Said I'd meet the team at Maple Leaf Gardens on Saturday afternoon.

"Well, Eddolls said, 'Gee, you'll have to speak to Tommy Ivan about that.' So I spoke to Ivan and he said, 'Well, that's a decision for the coach. Talk to Eddolls.' I found I was getting a real runaround so I shrugged and stayed put.

"After the game on Saturday, Ivan came into the dressing room and he said, 'Harry, how's the wife and family?' Well, I nearly blew my top. I brushed past him and went to the showers. Well, he waited for me to come out and started giving me the needle about being angry and not talking to him. I said, 'Tommy, I hate to be treated like a Boy Scout. All I wanted was a yes or no answer.' In Toronto and in Detroit, you always knew where you stood. Well, not in Chicago, not when I played there."

Watson joined the Hawks in December 1954, seven years after five of his good friends were dealt to the Hawks. Gus Bodnar was one of them.

"Do you know how we heard about the big trade that sent us to Chicago?" Gus Bodnar asks. "We heard it on the radio. This night the Leafs were going to the Old Mill Restaurant in Toronto, one of our regular haunts. We always went there on Monday night. And suddenly we hear about this big trade on the radio — five Leafs for two Blackhawks. Bob Goldham, Bud Poile, me, and two others, with Max Bentley coming the other way. We're all gone — the bunch of us. Gone. So we decided to have a hell of a party.

"And I remember some guy in the Old Mill that night made a smart-ass remark about Harry, who was having a great season in Toronto. Well, Harry grabbed that poor guy and threw him across the room. And there was one wall all enclosed in glass with some beautiful stuffed birds in behind. Harry threw this pecker with the big mouth right through the glass. And those birds took off. They flew! They might have been stuffed but they flew that night. All over the Old Mill."

Stanowski, chewing on his pipe, breaks out in laughter. "You're right, Gus. I saw it all. When Harry threw that ass though the glass the guy got to his feet covered in feathers. Looked like a turkey. What a night!"

I ask Watson, "Harry, as a left winger in the '50s you often had to watch out for the Rocket — Maurice Richard. Any major problems with him?"

"No, not really. I was a little bigger than the Rocket and I guess he knew I could fight when I was provoked. I recall one time with Chicago, we were playing against the Canadiens, and Henri Richard, the Pocket Rocket, started pushing and shoving Al Rollins, our goaltender. Then I saw the Rocket move right in and begin jabbing his stick at Rollins.

"I raced over and yanked the stick out of Rocket's hands and threw it aside. I told him, 'You stay out of this.' A few seconds later I see he's got his stick again and he starts jabbing it at Rollins. That made me mad so I barreled into him and put him hard up against the glass. And he said, 'I don' wan' you, 'arry. I don't wan' you.'" Watson laughs at the recollection.

"You ended your NHL career in Chicago, didn't you, Harry?"

"Yeah, I was getting ready to go to training camp in 1957 when I got a call from Tommy Ivan. He said, 'There are two playing coach's jobs open, one in Calgary and the other in Buffalo. Which one do you want?'

"I knew right then I wasn't going to be an NHLer anymore. So I told him I'd take the Buffalo job. It was a lot closer to home than Calgary."

5

Muldoon's Curse
Is Lifted

A Huge Victory
over Montreal

I T was the night of March 26, 1961 — almost four decades ago — when the Blackhawks stunned their opponents at Chicago Stadium in one of the greatest games ever played.

It was playoff time. The underdog Hawks faced the mighty Montreal Canadiens, who were looking for their sixth straight Stanley Cup — in the first round. The Hawks were given no chance. How could a third-place team unseat such a powerhouse: winners of the last five Stanley Cups; a team that had finished in first place for the fourth year in a row; a team with four scorers among the top ten (compared with none for Chicago); a team that had scored 56 more goals than the Blackhawks?

Somehow the Hawks managed to split the first two games in Montreal — a big surprise. But it would take a superb performance back on home ice for the Hawks to move ahead in the series.

A superb performance they got, especially from Glenn Hall in goal. His magical netminding had the fans stomping and cheering, and when the Hawks' Murray Balfour scored on Jacques Plante in the second period, the din in the old barn was deafening.

Hall and the Hawks nursed their one-goal lead through the third period. Hall's shutout was all but assured with only 16 seconds remaining on the clock, when there was a face-off deep in the Chicago zone. Montreal coach Toe Blake waved Plante to the bench and sent out an extra attacker.

Blake figured there was time for one or two shots against Hall. He counted on center Henri Richard to win the face-off. The puck was dropped and the Pocket Rocket snared it. He made a nifty little move, fired the puck at Hall, and the red light flashed. Tie score! The Chicago fans — many in shirtsleeves because of the intense heat inside the Stadium — howled in frustration.

The game went to overtime. Late in the extra period, Richard streaked in on a breakaway, only to have Hall come through with another scintillating save.

A second overtime period began. In this one, the Habs' Donnie Marshall batted a flying puck past Hall and the noisy crowd was shocked into silence. But referee Dalt McArthur waved his arms, signaling no goal. Marshall's stick was inches above his shoulder when he whacked the puck. Incensed, Blake shook his big fist at McArthur and shrieked obscenities at him.

The game continued into a third overtime period. After 11 minutes of play, Dickie Moore was sent to the penalty box and the Hawks raced away with the puck and stormed the Habs zone. From a scramble, Murray Balfour slid the rubber past Plante for the winning goal. Bedlam! The fans cheered for five minutes and littered the ice with programs and other debris. Then they roared again when they saw Montreal coach Toe Blake slip as he skidded across the ice in pursuit of referee McArthur. Enraged, Blake threw a wild punch at the official, an assault that would cost him a $2,000 fine — but strangely, no suspension.

The celebration of Balfour's goal didn't last long. Montreal stormed back to win game four by a 5–2 score and appeared to be back on track. But Glenn Hall registered back-to-back 3–0 shutouts in games five and six. The Habs' dynasty was over. It was one of hockey's greatest upsets.

The Hawks went on to eliminate Detroit in the finals, four games to two, and celebrated their first Stanley Cup triumph in twenty-three years. With marquee players like Hall, Pilote, Litzenberger, Hull, and Mikita in their prime, Hawk fans boldly predicted the champions would carry off several more Cups in the years ahead.

They never dreamed that one millennium would close and another begin, that four decades would pass without a drop of champagne from the coveted Cup spilling onto the lips of a Chicago player.

Fleming
Comes Through

A huge Stanley Cup goal scored by Reggie Fleming? You've got to be kidding.

No, sir, we're not kidding. And the Hawks haven't won a Stanley Cup since that long-ago evening.

It happened the night of April 16, 1961, at the Olympia in Detroit.

Muscular Reggie Fleming, a part-time player often ridiculed for his lack of skills, sent the Stanley Cup to Chicago for the first time in 23 seasons with a goal that lit a fire under the Hawks and turned the tide in the sixth game of the Stanley Cup finals.

"A lot of people laughed when we picked up Fleming from the Habs," said Chicago manager Tommy Ivan. "I wonder how many of them are laughing now."

In game five of the series, right winger Murray Balfour shattered his forearm. Next game, Fleming was moved up to the top line, where he shared the ice with Bobby Hull and Bill Hay.

The Hawks were trailing Detroit 1–0 in the second period when Chicago's Wayne Hicks was whistled off for hooking. Moments later, Len Lunde lost the puck to penalty killer Fleming, who barreled down the ice looking for a shorthanded goal. He was knocked off the puck by Vic Stasiuk, but he regained it when Stasiuk made a sloppy pass.

"I saw my chance and threw it in the short side," Fleming explained. "(Detroit goalie) Hank Bassen just stood there and watched it go in."

Fleming's goal brought the Hawks to life and they scored four more times to win in a romp, 5–1.

After the game Fleming spotted Canadiens public relations director Frank Selke, Jr., in the crowd and shouted, "I told you guys I'd play for a winner when you let me go. And all of you just laughed."

Fleming would score only 3 playoff goals in a twelve-season career. His first was always the one he savored the most.

Teammates Help Hull Win '62 Scoring Crown

I N 1962, the Blackhawks and the Rangers met in the final game of the season with the individual scoring crown up for grabs. Left winger Bobby Hull of Chicago was tied with New York right winger Andy Bathgate of the Rangers in the race for the Art Ross Trophy, both with 83 points. Hull, who notched 35 goals in the final 31 games, pulled ahead when he scored his 50th of the season early in the game, beating Ranger goalie Gump Worsley. He became only the third player ever to reach that plateau. But Bathgate, with 28 goals, picked up his 56th assist in the game to pull even.

Under NHL rules, if the scoring race ended in a deadlock Hull would capture the title because he'd scored more goals. If Bathgate was to win the scoring crown, he'd need one more point.

Hall of Famer Harry Howell, then New York's best defenseman, recalls the game vividly. What stands out most for him is how determined the Hawks were to keep Bathgate off the scoresheet.

"We tried desperately to get Andy one more point," Howell remembers. "That's all he needed to beat Hull. But the Hawks were all over Bathgate from the drop of the puck. Especially late in the game. Throughout the third period, they took one penalty after another. They didn't care if a Ranger scored — so long as it wasn't Andy. He never touched the puck. A Chicago player would grab his stick whenever he got near the puck and hang onto it. And happily serve a penalty. Then another Hawk would breathe down Andy's neck and do the same thing.

"With a couple of minutes to play, and the Rangers leading 4–1, Chicago coach Rudy Pilous sent Reggie Fleming, his most belligerent player, out to check Bathgate. Right off the face-off, Fleming pitchforked Andy into the ice, then he leaped on him. The referee threw up his arm, signaling a delayed penalty.

"We had the puck and we kept passing it back and forth, waiting for Andy to get up. There was still time for him to score. But he couldn't get up. So we tried for a whistle. We passed the puck to the Blackhawks, hoping they'd touch it and bring a whistle. But they wouldn't go near it. If it came close to their skates, they'd jump out of the way. It's the only game I ever played in where nobody wanted the puck.

"The referee's arm stayed up for what must have been a record time, the seconds slipped away and suddenly the game was over. Fleming and Bathgate were still wrestling around on the ice. By the time Bathgate struggled to his feet, Bobby Hull, the new scoring champion, was being congratulated by his teammates.

"I'm not saying he wouldn't have won the scoring crown anyway, but it wasn't captured in the best sporting tradition. If it hadn't been for Fleming's strong-arm tactics, and instructions from Pilous to smother Bathgate no matter what, the story might have had a different ending."

Bathgate recalls that it wasn't only Fleming, but also Eric Nesterenko, who gave him a lot of grief in that final game.

"They both piled into me and when I staggered to my feet at one point my stick was gone. It was in their hands. I managed to fall into the goal area without a stick, thinking maybe a shot would bounce into the net off my body. But it didn't happen. The Hawks gave me a classic mugging that night."

Who Bashed Balfour?

URING the 1960s, a fierce rivalry developed between the Blackhawks and the Toronto Maple Leafs. Each season, the fourteen regular-season meetings between these two teams could be counted on to deliver more than their share of physical play and bitter battles. And the teams were often scheduled to play back-to-back games over weekends, so a grudge triggered on a Saturday night at Maple Leaf Gardens would often be renewed twenty-four hours later at Chicago Stadium.

Two wild donnybrooks stand out — both of them resulting in nasty bench-clearing brawls. The first was in March 1961, and the second in December '63.

The 1961 episode erupted in the third period of a game at the Gardens. Defenseman Pierre Pilote, embarking on one of his patented end-to-end rushes, was speared by hard-checking Leaf winger Eddie "The Entertainer" Shack. Pilote responded by swinging his stick in the direction of Shack's bulbous nose, a rather inviting target. Shack's linemate Bert Olmstead immediately challenged Pilote and the battle was on.

While Pilote and Olmstead squared off, the Hawks' skating fire hydrant, Reggie Fleming, grappled with Leaf defenseman Larry Hillman. Shack, after satisfying himself that any wounds he'd suffered were not life-threatening, began to pick on Hawk centerman Stan Mikita. The players on the Chicago bench, seeing this mismatch, threw their sticks at the flailing Shack. Then, led by Bill Hay, they leaped onto the ice, followed immediately by the Leaf benchwarmers.

Fans at the rink, as well as those watching on national TV, chuckled as several of Toronto's finest slipped and slid around the ice in an effort to bring the brawl to an end. It was a rare sight to see police intervene in an on-ice dispute. Later, the NHL fined the main combatants appropriately for their indiscretions.

In December 1963, the Hawks again paid a visit to Maple Leaf

Gardens, bringing more than Christmas greetings. By this time, Fleming and Shack were involved in a long-running personal feud, and they were bent on inflicting as much pain on each other as possible.

In a radio interview before the game, Shack said, "Fleming is only dangerous when he's in behind a player — face-to-face he's a little cat who will run away." That set the stage for the evening's program.

The Leafs were leading 3–0 in the third period when Shack caught up to Fleming, planted his stick around the Hawk enforcer's thick neck, and quite rudely hauled him down. Fleming waited until his next shift before he got even — by using his stick to impale Shack, leaving his opponent gasping for air.

"Gotcha!" laughed Fleming as he skated directly to the penalty box to serve a five-minute sentence. That's when Bobby Baun, the Leafs' rugged defenseman, seeing his teammate in distress, tried to slug Fleming in the penalty box. Referee Frank Udvari ordered Fleming to the Chicago dressing room for his own safety.

That wasn't a good idea.

En route, Fleming had to cross the ice and skate past the Leaf bench. It was like asking him to swim through a swamp full of alligators. Leaf players came at him from all directions. He was challenged by Baun, by Larry Hillman, by Dick Duff. The benches cleared. Even Eddie Shack, who had seemed near death just moments earlier, made a miraculous recovery and dashed around, hoping to deliver a knuckle sandwich to some unsuspecting Hawk. Thirty minutes and sixteen penalties later, rugged Reggie finally staggered through the dressing-room door.

During the melee, Carl Brewer of the Leafs and Chicago's Murray Balfour found themselves battling on open ice. As they punched and clawed at each other, they moved toward the boards. Suddenly they fell through the open gate to the Leafs' bench, with Balfour on top. Somehow, Balfour suffered a nasty gash to his forehead, inflicted by a mysterious blow.

Hawks coach Billy Reay was livid; he accused Leaf trainer Bob Haggert of hitting Balfour. Haggert pleaded innocence. He said there were others close by, any one of whom might have clobbered Balfour. Balfour himself said, "It wasn't Brewer that hit me. It was either Haggert or Imlach."

"I didn't hit the so-and-so," protested Leaf coach Punch Imlach.

No one ever confessed to throwing the punch that cut Murray Balfour. A witness said he'd seen Haggert swinging his arm. Haggert maintained that a spectator had hit the Hawk and, although he recognized the individual, Haggert had no intention of naming him.

During the incident, Chicago's Howie Young had skated to the Leaf bench, peered into the seats, and asked a familiar-looking gent sitting directly behind the Leaf bench if he'd been involved. "Sure, I was down there," said the spectator. "So what?"

"You're not so tough," said Young. "Come on down here."

The spectator — Toronto Argonaut football star Dick Shatto — jumped from his seat. He was poised to accept Young's challenge when a policeman's quick intervention stopped him.

When it was all over, the players on both teams and their coaches were assessed a record amount in fines. The papers called the game a renewal of the teams' "sizzling vendetta." Even coaches Reay and Imlach (who'd fired Reay as Leaf coach years before) exchanged profanities publicly after the game.

Recently, over lunch with Carl Brewer, I asked, "What really happened that night? Who threw the punch that cut Balfour?" Carl chuckled and said, "It wasn't me. I had my head under the bench and couldn't get at him. Besides, I was recovering from a broken arm and was worried about throwing punches with it. It was Dick Shatto who jumped in and punched him."

Why would he do that?

"Why? Because I was his son's favorite hockey player and he thought I was getting the worst of it."

Mahovlich for Sale
— Or Is He?

I N *The Globe and Mail*, respected Canadian sports columnist Scott Young called it H-O-K-U-M. He also called it bunkum, nonsense, guile, delusion, gullery, bluff, hanky panky, sham, make-believe, spoof, hoax, bamboozle, gerrymandering, and humbug.

One sports editor referred to it as "a game of highball roulette."

What were they talking about? If you guessed the great million-dollar non-deal for Frank Mahovlich, you can go straight to the head of the hockey class.

Friday, October 5, 1962, was the eve of the annual All-Star Game that kicked off each new season. Harold Ballard, Stafford Smythe, and John Bassett had just purchased the Toronto Maple Leafs, and Ballard was downing drinks with the owner of the Blackhawks, Big Jim Norris. When midnight rolled around, Norris made Ballard an offer.

"I hear you fellows are having trouble signing the big kid Mahovlich," he began. "I'd pay a lot of money to have that kind of a problem."

"How much money?" Ballard asked.

"I'd give you a million dollars for him," Norris countered.

Ballard almost dropped his drink. "A million? For a hockey player? Jim, for a million, you've got him. He's yours."

The two men shook hands on a deal that took them mere seconds to consummate. Norris stood up and peeled ten $100 bills from a roll in his pocket. He handed them to Ballard.

"A down payment," he said. "I'll get the rest of the money to you tomorrow morning."

Ballard wrote out a note: "We except (sic) on behalf of the Toronto Maple Leafs." He signed the scrap of paper and handed it to Jack Amell, a Gardens executive, who also signed the paper.

Norris then told Tommy Ivan, his general manager, to get on the phone to Chicago and tell the team's publicity director to release the news to the media immediately. Bulletins were flashed by the major news agencies into newsrooms and radio stations from coast to coast. The sale of Mahovlich for $1 million was electrifying news.

Meanwhile, back in Room 11-268 of the Royal York Hotel, Stafford Smythe had made an appearance. "This will put the World Series off the sports pages tomorrow," he crowed, treating the matter as a joke. Not once did he say, "Guys, we're all just kidding, right?"

Toronto coach Punch Imlach didn't think there was anything funny about what went down. He refused to shake hands with Norris to help cement the deal, choosing instead to go home, disturbed and disgusted with what he'd seen and heard.

The next morning, Tommy Ivan appeared at Maple Leaf Gardens with a big grin on his face and a check for a million dollars in his pocket. He was wondering how he was going to fit both Mahovlich and Bobby Hull — the game's two best left wingers — into his lineup. "I might have to bench Hull once in a while," he kidded a friend.

Ushered into a meeting room, Ivan tried to hand the check, signed by Norris, to the Leaf triumvirate of Ballard, Smythe, and Bassett. None of them would take it. By this time, former Leaf owner Conn Smythe had thrown his two cents' worth into the mix. He'd blistered his son and the others, saying they were making fools of themselves if they agreed to sell Mahovlich.

The Leaf brass politely told Ivan to take his boss's money and leave.

"We've decided that Mahovlich is not for sale," they said. "Not even for a million dollars."

Meanwhile, Frank Mahovlich was waiting in a nearby room. He was there to talk contract with Imlach. When asked about the deal, he said, "It sure sounds like a lot of guff to me."

But it was no guff to Jim Norris. "It was a straight deal and the Leafs welshed on it," he said. "Simple as that."

Scott Young's *Globe and Mail* column, in which he mocked the shenanigans of the Leaf braintrust, cost him heavily. At the time, he held a second job as host of *Hockey Night in Canada*. Shortly after his column appeared, he was told he was no longer welcome in that position. Seems the Leafs had the final say on who could work on the hockey telecasts.

Young ended his column in a typically humorous vein. He wrote:

On the day that the Leafs sell Mahovlich (now 24), when he is worth a million dollars to any hockey man who has it to spare:

- The sun will rise in the West;
- Eddie Shack will be named Miss Body Beautiful of the half-century;
- Sonny Liston will read the lesson in Timothy Eaton Memorial Church;
- Punch Imlach will appear in a television commercial plugging that greasy kid stuff.

Hall's Incredible Streak

IN modern-day hockey it's customary for a team to employ two, three, sometimes half a dozen goaltenders over the course of a grueling NHL season. But just thirty years ago or so, teams relied solely on one man to play between the pipes. Hard to believe, but in that six-team era, the seventh-best goalie in hockey toiled in the minors.

No team relied more heavily on their goaltender than the Chicago Blackhawks of the late '50s and early '60s. During those years, Glenn Hall was a durable superstar for the Hawks. Season after season, he never missed a game.

Back in 1955, the Detroit Red Wings tapped Hall to replace

Terry Sawchuk in goal. He played every game that season, and his streak was unbroken when he came to the Hawks in 1957. The games piled up and the records began to fall: 300 consecutive games, then 400 and even 500. What's more, Hall played without a mask, risking cuts and concussions with every start.

He did miss a few preseason games, however: every fall, he'd report to camp as late as possible.

"I'm painting my barn" was his excuse when the manager called, pleading with him to report.

"Glenn's either got the best-painted barn in Saskatchewan or he's the slowest painter on earth," the manager would tell reporters.

After he retired, Hall would ask, "Why would any goalie report to camp on time in those days? Just to stand there facing shots from Bobby or Dennis Hull. Those guys would drive you crazy."

When he finally reported and a new season began, Hall was all business. He'd strap on the pads, throw up his pregame meal, wrestle the team trainer around the dressing room for ten or fifteen minutes to steady his nerves, then announce he was ready to play.

And how he played! On most nights, healthy or hurt, he performed superbly. With Hall tending goal, the Hawks were always in the game. Two more points were always within reach.

"I had to play well," he once said. "I could never play poorly. As a goalie, I set a standard and to play below that standard was simply unacceptable. I forced myself to play well."

On the night of November 7, 1962, Chicago played host to the Boston Bruins. On this night there was no wrestling before the game. Hall's lower back, wracked by excruciating pain, would not permit it. But when the Hawks took the ice that night, Hall was standing calmly in his crease.

In the opening minutes of play, Boston's Murray Oliver shot the puck at Hall and it flew right between his legs. Hall's back had tightened up, and he simply could not bend over to stop the shot.

He skated slowly to the Chicago bench, whispered a few words to coach Rudy Pilous, and headed for the dressing room. His departure, in his 503rd consecutive game, brought to an end a string of more than 30,000 consecutive minutes of goaltending.

It's one hockey record that will never be broken. Ask any of the modern-day millionaire goalies if they'd like to play in every game for seven years and the answer is predictable: "You crazy, man? No goalie could survive a workload like that and still be sane."

Glenn Hall did — and is.

Pilous Had Personality

WHEN Rudy Pilous took over the Chicago Blackhawks coaching reins in January 1958, his prospects for success were abysmal. The Hawks had finished at the very bottom of the NHL standings in eight of the previous ten seasons.

People can say that Pilous got lucky — that Bobby Hull, Stan Mikita, Glenn Hall, and Pierre Pilote would have changed all that, and turned losses into wins, no matter who was hired to coach them. But the man behind the bench deserves some credit, too — a whole lot of it.

In his six seasons with the Blackhawks, Pilous led his team into the playoffs five times, guided them to the Stanley Cup finals twice, and was there to help them celebrate a Stanley Cup victory in 1961 — the Hawks' first taste of champagne in twenty-three years. They haven't put their mitts on it since.

Why did Pilous leave? He was pushed — fired — after the 1962–63 season when the Red Wings eliminated the Hawks in the Stanley Cup semifinals, four games to two. Manager Tommy Ivan didn't consider the Hawks' second-place finish in the regular season — one point behind Toronto — to be good enough to keep Pilous around.

"For some reason, Ivan never liked me," Pilous said of his dismissal. "He would never have hired me in the first place if Jim Norris hadn't all but ordered him to. Offered me $9,000 to sign.

Hell, I was making more than that coaching Junior hockey. Finally, Mr. Norris himself got involved, got on the phone to me and hired me for a fair chunk of money. But I knew I'd be gone at the first sign of a letdown or a slump. People told me Ivan was afraid I'd take his job one day. And later on, it didn't help that Bobby Hull and Stan Mikita complained about me being too tough and cold and bad for team morale."

Years later, while serving as player-coach of the Winnipeg Jets in the WHA, Hull admitted he'd been wrong about his former boss. "I was still a kid when I played for Rudy in Chicago," Hull admitted. "Didn't know much about coaching then. Now I've been a coach myself and I know what he was up against. Rudy has moved with the times, become less rigid. That's why I wanted him to coach the Winnipeg Jets."

Pilous had more than coaching smarts. He had an abundance of personality. He loved the limelight and he knew how to entertain. Whenever Chicago played at the Montreal Forum, fans serenaded him with shouts of "Pil-oo, Pil-oo." He would egg them on, then doff his hat and flash them a smile.

At sports banquets he was in demand as a speaker, regaling his audience with stories told in a dozen dialects — German, Irish, Jewish, Russian, and French, to mention a few.

"Some people say I was a better storyteller than I was a coach," he told reporter Earl McRae. "But why can't a person be funny, be entertaining, and still know his job?"

Why indeed?

One of his favorite stories was about his Junior team in St. Catharines — and how he pulled his goaltender late in a playoff game with St. Mike's. It's a common ploy, of course, but Pilous did it when the face-off was in the St. Catharines zone.

"My own players thought I was nuts," he said. "So did most of the fans, who started to leave the rink in disgust. But the strategy worked when the opposing players raced toward the empty net, and a kid named Hugh Barlow sped away with the puck and scored on St. Mike's goalie Gerry McNamara with 28 seconds left on the clock. We went on to win that game. Then we stayed hot and captured the Memorial Cup."

Hull and Espo

BY 1964 Chicago general manager Tommy Ivan and coach Billy Reay had shaped the Blackhawks into a potential NHL dynasty. Contributing to the cause was a young man who would go on to become one of the greatest scorers of all time.

"When I got called up to Chicago," Phil Esposito recalls, "the second or third game I played was in New York. And Billy Reay said to me, 'I'm going to change the lines around. You're going to center Bobby Hull and Chico Maki.' Now, Bill Hay had been playing center with Bobby and Murray Balfour. What a break that was for me. Bobby and I and Chico started to click. It was unbelievable how we just kept scoring and playing great."

Dennis Hull recalls that unstoppable combination. "Bobby and Phil and Chico. What a dominant line! Phil had only been around a short time and he had three 20-goal seasons. One year he scored 27. We could all see that Phil was going to be a magnificent player. And why Tommy Ivan couldn't see that borders on tragedy — it was almost beyond belief."

In 1967 Ivan traded Esposito to the Boston Bruins in what is invariably called "the most lopsided deal in NHL history." Esposito, Ken Hodge, and Fred Stanfield went to the lowly Bruins for center Pit Martin, defenseman Gilles Marotte, and goaltender Jack Norris. Boston fans rejoiced for the next ten years.

"Yeah, they traded me," says Phil. "And it was Bobby Hull who told me about the deal."

It had been a frustrating three seasons for Esposito. It started when he first came up from the minors. His salary had been $8,000 in St. Louis; when he was "promoted" to the Hawks he actually had to take a pay cut — to $7,500, the NHL minimum. Then there was the time Hull came across the dressing room at the Montreal Forum the night of Phil's first game and said, "Hi, Phil, glad to have you aboard," and somebody else shouted, "Hey, we got a wop with us!" And what about all those games in which he'd been mostly a benchwarmer? And the contract disputes with Tommy Ivan that left Espo feeling more than once that he'd been shortchanged? Then there was the feeling that he'd been branded as a lousy playoff performer.

At first, the trade was a slap in the kisser, especially when he was headed to Boston, a team that hadn't made the playoffs since 1959. But the more he thought about it, the less Esposito regretted leaving the Blackhawks, the team he'd cheered since boyhood. It was obvious he was the principal figure in the deal, the one player everyone was talking about. Ironically, he had to be dealt to another NHL team before his name was all over the Chicago papers and people were calling for interviews.

In Boston, Esposito would get to play with a phenom named Orr, he'd been promised a hike in salary, and Milt Schmidt wanted to make him an assistant captain. "I made up my mind within days of the deal that I'd show the Hawks and the Bruins — in fact, I'd show the whole damn world — what a hockey player Phil Esposito can be."

Fifty-One Gifts for Hull

WHERE do you find room in a modest three-bedroom bungalow for a ton of unexpected gifts?

Bobby Hull didn't know. If the gifts kept coming — 51 at a time — he said he might have to rent a storage locker.

On March 12, 1966, after Hull scored his record-breaking 51st goal of the season against the Rangers' Cesare Maniago, a Chicago disc jockey immediately urged listeners to send presents — 51 of them — to the Golden Jet.

Delivery men began arriving at the Hull household to hand over 51 chocolate hockey pucks, 51 litter bags for Hull's cattle, 51 puck-shaped steaks, a hockey stick with 51 diamonds imbedded in it, 51 weeks' worth of tobacco, 51 frozen TV dinners, and, among other things, 51 mops. Hull's wife Joanne received 51 roses, 51 pairs of stockings, and a gold bracelet with 51 charms.

In the mail was a certificate for 51 car washes and the use of a new car for 51 days. Lawyers offered $51 worth of legal advice (good for about 15 minutes in those days) and a plumber gave $51 in services.

Chicago grocers donated 51 cans of fruit juice, 51 hot dogs, 51 pancakes, and a number of other handy items — all in batches of 51.

Chicago Bears linebacker Dick Butkus sent Hull his jersey — Number 51.

A modeling agency offered to send over 51 models who were eager to give Hull 51 kisses — each.

"I gave Joanne 51 seconds to decide on that one," Bobby said. "And she still has 50 left."

Hull's 51st goal — the record-setter — came at 5:34 of the third period on a long shot that was partially screened by Eric Nesterenko, who darted across the goal crease in front of Maniago just as Hull's slapper arrived at the net. For a few seconds, Hull did not raise his arms to celebrate his feat because he wasn't sure he'd scored. But 22,000 fans screamed in delight.

"I had to wait," Hull would say. "Eric jabbed at Maniago's stick when he swept by and I thought perhaps he'd deflected it in."

When the official scorer credited Hull, he skated over to the glass, sidestepping programs and hats that had been tossed on the ice, and blew a kiss to his wife Joanne. Impishly he reached down, grabbed a hat and shoved it on his head, triggering another huge roar from the crowd.

At the end of the 4–2 Chicago win, Hull and Stan Mikita embraced each other and skated off together. Hull told reporters, "I'm glad I scored it in Chicago where the people have been so wonderful to us." He was asked to kiss his wife several times for the photographers and he happily obliged, but not before slipping his dentures into place. "You guys are always trying to catch me without my teeth in," he laughed. "But not this time."

For almost an hour, still in his uniform, he answered questions from the media. When he finally showered and left the building, he spent another forty-five minutes signing autographs for his fans.

"If they're good enough to put me up on a bit of a pedestal, the least I can do is try to return the kindness," he said.

Cesare Maniago, the Ranger goalie who, as a Leaf, was also the victim of Geoffrion's 50th goal, shrugged off Hull's record-breaking blast: "Nesterenko lifted my stick when he went by or I might have had it. I'm already in the books for giving up Geoffrion's goal. Why should I worry about Hull's?"

Hull's Record-Breaking Goal

WHEN Maurice "Rocket" Richard scored his 50th goal in the 50th game of the 1944–45 season, Bobby Hull was a six-year-old living in Pointe Anne, Ontario.

Eventually, the Rocket's record was tied by another Montrealer, Boom Boom Geoffrion, who scored his 50th in the 1960–61 season. Fans of the Rocket were quick to point out that the NHL had been playing a 70-game schedule since 1949, and Geoffrion therefore enjoyed a lot more ice time — he played in 64 games in 1960–61 — in which to score his 50 goals. Geoffrion's backers countered with the suggestion that the Rocket's mark was set during wartime, when many of the best NHL players were in military service.

By the time Geoffrion tied the Rocket's record, Bobby Hull was a scoring whiz in his own right with the Chicago Blackhawks. His rink-long rushes and sizzling slap shots had already earned him a colorful nickname, "The Golden Jet."

Hull electrified an entire generation of fans with his skill, style, and charm. He still reigns as the greatest left winger in the history of hockey.

"I loved to pick up the puck behind Glenn Hall in the Chicago net. If I could go the length of the rink and put that puck in the other team's net, more power to me. And if I could pass it off to a teammate and get a return pass and put it in, so much the better. And often Pierre Pilote — I loved Pierre Pilote — would be on defense when I started a rush. He'd holler, 'Hold on, Bobby, let me touch the puck. Then when you score I'll get an easy assist.'"

Pierre Pilote says, "People started to jump right out of their seats when Bobby led a rush. And all of a sudden . . . *whump*, he'd let go a shot and the goalie would have to try and stop it. They hated to touch that puck when Bobby shot it."

Don Cherry says, "I remember (Boston goalie) Gerry Cheevers talking about Bobby's shot. He said there were times he hoped it would go in the net so it wouldn't hit him. There's guys in the league now who can really hum a puck, but when Hull was on stride and stepped into one, boy, it was deadly. There wasn't anybody who had a harder shot. He was unbelievable."

"People in Chicago considered Bobby to be the greatest athlete in the city when he was there," brother Dennis says. "You could have asked Gale Sayers or Dick Butkus or some of the Bulls — and I've been out with them — and they would have agreed that Bobby was the marquee player in Chicago."

In 1961–62 everything jelled for the Golden Jet. Hull became the NHL's third 50-goal man, tying the mark held by the Rocket and Boom Boom. Hull followed up with seasons of 31, 43, and 39 goals, and then, in 1965–66 he tied the record again, scoring his 50th in a game versus Detroit. A horrible slump followed, during which the Blackhawks were shut out in three consecutive games.

Finally on March 12, 1966, playing at home against the Rangers and with the Hawks trailing 2–1 in the third period, Hull skated into the New York zone. Inside the blue line he took a drop pass from Lou Angotti and almost fanned on one of his patented slap shots.

"It's true," he said later. "I got the heel of my stick on the puck and it turned out to be one of the worst slap shots I ever took. But Eric Nesterenko skated in front of Ranger goalie Cesare Maniago just as I let 'er go, blocked his view, and the puck slipped into the corner of the net."

That was goal number 51 — a new NHL record. The 22,000 fans at Chicago Stadium gave Hull an ovation that lasted ten minutes. "I'll never forget it," Hull said. "I had goose bumps all over me. It was one of the most thrilling moments I've ever experienced." Hull finished the season with 54 goals in 65 games.

During 1968–69, the second year of the expanded twelve-team league, Hull exploded for 58 goals in 74 games, another new standard.

If, at that time, someone had predicted that one of Hull's sons would one day surpass his feats, that person would have been greeted with derisive laughter. "There's only one Golden Jet," he would have been told.

The Blackhawks management must have agreed. In 1988, when the Calgary Flames were shopping a young Brett Hull around, Chicago was among the teams who passed on a chance to acquire him.

The St. Louis Blues took a chance on him, and within a few years, Brett would post seasons of 70, 72, and 86 goals. Along the way he earned a nickname, "The Golden Brett," that was fitting of his hockey lineage. During the 1999–2000 season, playing for the Dallas Stars, Brett Hull tied his famous père's NHL career goal total of 610.

Bobby and Brett Hull are the only father-son combination to have their names engraved on the Hart Trophy.

Creating the
Curved Stick

BOBBY Hull's slap shot was devastating. And it became even more deadly in the '60s, when he began using a stick with a curved blade. Sometimes the shot would dip in midflight, causing the goalie facing the missile to panic and fan on the shot.

Historians say that others — Andy Bathgate, for one — used a gently curved blade before Hull. And they may be right. But Hull credits his teammate Stan Mikita for the invention.

"Like many great discoveries it happened by accident," Mikita says. "We were at the end of a practice one day at the Chicago Stadium and my stick cracked in the blade. I noticed it now had a little curve in the blade where it had cracked. I hadn't brought a spare stick from the dressing room, which was downstairs at the Stadium. I was too tired to go fetch another stick so I used the broken one. I took a couple of shots at the boards and noticed that the puck made an unusual sound when it hit. That made me inquisitive. Why did the puck sound different? And why did the puck feel like it was moving a little faster off the blade?"

After practice, Mikita and Hull took some sticks from the team's stick rack, heated the blades and then placed them under a radiator. They applied enough force to bend the blades into a banana-shape and then experimented with them on the ice. They were amazed at the results. Not only did pucks fly with more velocity, but passing the puck with the banana blade resulted in quicker, more accurate passes.

Some players of that era pooh-poohed the innovation. Dave Keon, among others, tried the curved blade and tossed it aside. But many jumped on the bandwagon, from players in old-timers' leagues to small fry, and even goaltenders. Within months, it was hard to find a straight-bladed stick in any sporting goods store.

In 1999, Hall of Famer Andy Bathgate claimed that he was the originator of the curved blade. "I used a curved blade when I was a kid playing road hockey in Winnipeg," he attests. "When I turned pro with the Rangers I would heat the blade of my sticks with hot water and put them under a door in the dressing room. But the problem was, in time the blades would straighten out. So Northland, my stick supplier, added fiberglass to the blades and that kept the hook in place.

"I remember Stan Mikita grabbing a couple of my sticks from our trainer in New York. He got two goals and three assists in his next game using those sticks. I know I was using a hooked stick three or four years before Mikita and Hull came into the league."

"Whoa!" says Mikita when told of Bathgate's claim. "Andy's getting up there in age and you know what they say, the mind is the second thing to go. I never saw Andy using a hooked stick and I don't recall grabbing any in New York." (This is somewhat of a contradiction to a statement Mikita made in his 1969 auto-biography *I Play to Win*: "Of course we weren't the first to use a curved stick. Apparently Andy Bathgate, who played for many years with the New York Rangers, also had tried one.")

Tom Nease, former president of the sporting goods company CCM, backs Bathgate. In a February 1999 letter to *The Hockey News*, he wrote: "As much as I admire Stan Mikita for the skill and flair he brought to the NHL, Andy Bathgate can correctly claim fame as the player who introduced the curved blade to the NHL. I became president of CCM in 1962 and I remember visiting Maple Leaf Gardens with our equipment man, George Parsons. One morning in the early 1960s, we chatted with Bathgate and watched as he took hot water–soaked blades on a few sticks and carefully bent them under the dressing room doors. It was definitely later that Mikita, then Bobby Hull, started to use the curved stick."

Perfect Pit
Spoke His Mind

WHEN the Chicago Blackhawks acquired Hubert "Pit" Martin from the Boston Bruins in May 1967, they didn't know they were getting an opinionated chatterbox. In 1969, Martin was asked about the Hawks' last-place finish the season before — despite a 107-point season by Bobby Hull and 97 more from Stan Mikita — and he was quick to take the bait.

"The problem in Chicago is a total lack of direction," he said. "There is no leadership from the owners, the general manager, or the coach. And when they're not concerned, the players aren't concerned.

"Then there's the matter of a star conflict. The Hawks have one big star (Hull scored 58 goals and finished second to Phil Esposito in the scoring race) and another fairly big star (Mikita finished fourth in scoring) and the club seems to be set up to make them happy. The rest of us simply don't matter."

Martin's candid comments were music to the ears of reporter Bob Verdi, who scribbled down notes of their conversation, knowing they made good copy and might even cause turmoil in the Hawks' front office.

But it was hard to knock the results. In 1969–70 there was an immediate improvement in team play and hustle. After a dreadful start (thanks largely to the absence of Bobby Hull, who missed the first twelve games due to a contract dispute), the Hawks began to shine. Rookies Tony Esposito, Cliff Koroll, and Keith Magnuson came into their own, and the club — with 45 victories — finished in a tie with Boston for the East Division championship.

Goaltender Esposito racked up a modern-day, and rookie, record of 15 shutouts, helping the team improve by 22 points and leap from last place to first in just one season. Martin backed up his words with action, scoring 30 goals and capturing the Bill Masterton Trophy, which is awarded to the NHL player who best exemplifies qualities of perseverance, dedication, and sportsmanship. The voters couldn't have made a better choice.

Three years later, Verdi had more to write about after Martin popped off again.

"I just heard about the contract Bobby Clarke signed with the Flyers. He gets $100,000 for five years, plus other perks. Sure he carries that Flyer team. But I'm doing a competent job with a winning team — Philadelphia hasn't won anything yet — and I make a third of what Clarke earns. And I don't have a long-term contract." This observation came after Bill Reay, Martin's coach, told the media, "I think Martin should be an All-Star."

"After five years as a Blackhawk I still don't feel like I'm a vital part of the club," Martin stated matter-of-factly. "Billy Reay is one of my biggest boosters but they could trade me tomorrow. Maybe if I was a good player on a weaker club — like Clarke — I'd be worth more money. Is that right? Is it fair?

"If I talk about a long-term contract with Tommy Ivan, he gives me the story about becoming complacent. I'm conscientious. I'm a professional. I'm not going to let up. Don't they realize that?"

Verdi would call Martin's candid assessment of the Chicago organization the "State-of-the-Blackhawks Message."

"There is no discipline with the Blackhawks," Verdi quoted Martin as saying. "Players do as they please. Several players have one ambition and that is to score goals, no matter how many the opposition scores while they are on the ice. There's a total lack of spirit.

"Some of our players don't react after a victory. In fact, they're unhappy if they haven't scored. On the other hand, after a defeat, they're quite content if they've scored a goal or two."

Martin expressed surprise at the disinterest of management and how the stars were allowed to go their own way, to be late for practice if they felt like it, to take a different flight to a road game if they had a personal appearance scheduled. "If you're part of a team, you're part of a team," he said. "Simple as that."

How did the players and management react to Martin's critical barbs?

Billy Reay immediately laid down some long-overdue common-sense rules and guidelines. The rookies, role players, and grinders applauded Martin's statements and began working as never before. Stan Mikita took a few shots at Martin, calling him "Perfect Pit."

Martin shrugged and said, "I can live with that. It doesn't bother me."

Out on a Ledge

DON "Sockeye" Uren, a former Chicago trainer, swears the story happened just the way he tells it.

"I was the trainer for the Blackhawks back in the '60s and some of the Hawks loved to make me the butt of their jokes. I remember one time we flew into New York for a game with the Rangers and we bedded down on the eighteenth floor of a Manhattan hotel. I was about to enter my room when one of the players called me down the hall.

"'Sockeye,' he pleaded. 'Help me out, will ya? Somebody's played a joke on me and placed my shoes on a ledge just outside my window. I'm terrified of heights and I'm scared to death of climbing out there to retrieve them. Would you please do it for me, please?'

"Well, I looked over the scene and sure enough the shoes were out on the ledge. Heights never bothered me. And the ledge was pretty wide. So I climbed out and started crawling along the ledge towards the shoes. Just as I was reaching for them, the window flew up in the room ahead of me, a hand reached out and snatched the shoes away. At the same time I heard a noise behind me. Someone had slammed shut the window I'd just crawled through.

"That's when I knew that I'd been conned — it was all a

bizarre practical joke. I was trapped out there with no way back. I didn't panic. Still, eighteen floors is a long way up — or down, depending on your point of view. I might have been able to break the window, but there was flying glass to consider. I decided to wait the boys out, let them have their fun. Surely, they'd let me back in a minute or two.

"Then I heard the sirens. When I looked down, the street below was filling up with police cars, fire trucks, and an ambulance. Within minutes, a big Irish cop eased open the nearest window and began talking to me in a soothing voice. 'You've got a lot to live for, son,' said the cop.

"'I couldn't agree with you more, officer,' I told him, reaching for his hand.

"Back in the room, I saw a man in a white coat holding a needle. He talked to the policeman about giving me a shot to calm me down. Another man held an article of clothing that looked suspiciously like a straitjacket. I kept insisting it was all a gag, that I'd been the victim of a practical joke. I repeated my story all the way to the police station. But nobody believed me.

"At the station I told the head cop that the whole matter could be cleared up with a call to one or two of the Chicago players. They would certainly help me out of this fix.

"The call was promptly made and the players contacted. You guessed it! The players said they didn't know of any practical joke. What's more, they'd never heard of Sockeye Uren. Goodbye.

"I began to perspire. I used all my powers of persuasion. I explained how hockey players were notorious practical jokers. I told them the players had once chained me naked to a bus railing outside of Maple Leaf Gardens in Toronto. I agreed that leaving me on a window ledge eighteen floors up was carrying a practical joke to the limit and I promised it would never happen again. Finally, they decided to release me.

"I raced back to the hotel, gnashing my teeth. I couldn't wait to give those jokers a tongue-lashing. I was so mad I was ready to crack a few heads together.

"When I got back to the eighteenth floor, it was deserted. I found a note under my door. It said:

"'Dear Sockeye:
Where have you been? We wanted you to come to the movies
with us but somebody said you'd stepped out for some fresh air.
See you later.
The boys.'"

Sockeye's Seen It All

D ON "Sockeye" Uren is a little-known, but laugh-provoking, character who has been around the hockey scene a long time as a trainer and practice goalie in Toronto and Chicago, and as a trainer for the Buffalo Sabres.

In his time he's seen blood, broken bones, and hockey injuries that would sicken the squeamish.

"One of the goriest sights I ever encountered happened one night in Chicago. Eddie Shack of the Leafs sailed through goalie Glenn Hall's crease skates flying high. Glenn went down on his knees and one of Shack's skates sliced Glenn's leg open just about the knee.

"I ran out and uncovered the wound. It was incredible! Somehow the skate had cut a triangle of flesh out of Hall's upper leg. The team doctor and I grabbed the loose flesh, like you would a chunk of meat, and it came away. We wrapped it in gauze and I rushed into the training room and dipped it in an alcohol solution until Glenn could be brought in.

"The doctor put the chunk of flesh back in place and stitched Glenn up. It was a remarkable piece of work — I'd never seen anything like it. Glenn was out about two weeks but he might have been hobbled for months if it hadn't been for such quick action.

"Hall also was involved in the second-worst injury I ever saw. At Maple Leaf Gardens one night, Ron Ellis took a wicked slap shot that hit Glenn flush in the face. His face was a mess.

I rushed onto the ice, and before we got Glenn to the bench I'd used up every piece of gauze in my bag. There was blood everywhere!

"The cut ran from his forehead, down his nose, and under his eye. It took twenty-six stitches, but again Glenn wasn't the type of player to let such an ugly wound keep him out of action.

"What suffering that man has gone through, and what a class guy he is! For twenty years he battled injuries, nerves, and immense pressure. And that's no bull about him getting sick before the games, and often between periods. He'd bring *everything* up.

"The only remedy we ever found that helped him was straight from Sockeye's medical book. Believe it or not, we started wrestling each other an hour or two before game time.

"Glenn would be Sweet Daddy Siki and I'd be Bulldog Brower, and we'd clear the dressing room and go at it hammer and tongs. Anybody who saw us in there thought we were nuts. We'd beat the heck out of each other, and after a while Glenn would call a halt and say he felt better and was ready to suit up.

"It was the only way we discovered to release Glenn's pregame tension. But it sure was rough on me, because I'd often be battered and bruised."

Sockeye recalled some other injuries, and winced as he described them.

"Stan Mikita suffered a freak accident one night. Doug Mohns fired a pass to Stan, but the puck zoomed straight up and caught Stan in the ear. His ear was hanging by a thread. The doctor counted ninety-six stitches that night, and yet Stan, despite great pain, insisted on playing the next night against Toronto.

"I rigged up an ear protector and attached it to his helmet. Actually, it was the cup from an athletic supporter, filled with cotton. But it did the trick and Stan scored three goals, including the winner, against the Leafs. Anybody who says hockey players aren't the toughest pro athletes around doesn't know beans!"

Who was the toughest, most durable of the players he's trained?

"Bobby Hull," he shot back. "No question. And Glenn Hall, too. But Hull was something else. Remember the time somebody broke his jaw? At the hospital the doctor had to punch out two teeth just to get inside and work on his jaw. The doctor told him he was in bad shape and wouldn't be able to play for an indefinite time.

"The next day I was amazed when Bobby showed up at the rink. His face was all puffed out and he looked awful. He asked me to fix him up with a special helmet and mask, and I told him he was nuts. But he insisted, so we rigged something up and he played in the next game.

"He couldn't eat because of his wired jaw, so I bought a blender and carried it with me for a month. Bobby's pregame steak went into the blender, and somehow we got it into him. In hotels and airports, I was forever ordering milkshakes and he'd sip them through a straw.

"I've seen Bobby play on an ankle so badly twisted he could hardly walk. And with a back that doubled him up with pain. And the worst, perhaps, was the broken nose he picked up in a playoff series with Detroit one year. He looked like he'd been hit with a sledgehammer. His eyes were black and swollen and we had to stuff his nostrils with cotton.

"Again the doctor told him he was in no condition to play. But Bobby surprised everybody — well, not everybody, because I knew what he was thinking. He flew into Detroit and played against the Wings. We lost, but Bobby scored the hat trick and he played with no protection over his face.

"Let me just finish with one little story that illustrates why Bobby, to me, is one of the classiest guys I've ever met. The Chicago Stadium is in the middle of a ghetto, and the little black kids were always hanging around. Some were good kids, others would slit your throat. They asked me one day if Bobby would come out and say hello to them. I told Bobby and he said sure, he'd be glad to.

"Well, when he saw how impoverished they were, and when they asked him to walk down the street and visit their church, he couldn't refuse. Few whites walk around that district, but Bobby wasn't afraid. He was gone for hours and I was really worried, because we had a game that night and he'd already missed his normal dinner hour.

"Finally, he called and said, 'Sockeye, maybe you could order me a small steak and salad and I'll eat it at the rink. These kids seemed to enjoy my visit, and it's tough just to say hello and goodbye. I'll be back soon.' And he was. But what an amazing guy!"

Here's another yarn from the endless collection of Don "Sockeye" Uren.

"Again, this goes back to the days when I was with Chicago. We were coming back from Boston, on our way to a game in Toronto, where I'd purchased a long, heavy chain — you know, the kind they use to secure boats to a dock. Well, this was for Ed Van Impe's boat.

"Now, let's start by saying those Chicago players delighted in playing practical jokes, especially if I was the target. We got off the plane in Toronto, and boarded a bus for the Royal York Hotel. On the way to the hotel, some of the boys asked me to show them the chain, so I unpacked it.

"Geez, if I'd known what they had in mind I'd never have done so. They grabbed the chain and then they grabbed me. You won't believe this, but they stripped me naked on that bus, and I watched in horror as they hurled my clothes, piece by piece, out the bus window. All I had left was a light topcoat, which I hauled around me. Then they took the chain and wrapped it around me until I couldn't move. There was a padlock on one end and they padlocked me to the seat.

"By this time we'd reached the Royal York, and I was hollering at them to let me go. But they all got off, and one of them calmly dropped the key to the padlock down the grillwork of the nearest rain drain. I was pop-eyed.

"They instructed the bus driver to take me to Maple Leaf Gardens, where I'd normally go anyway to store the equipment. He did, then he had to go in and find Doug Moore, one of the Gardens' engineers. Finally, someone took pity on me. Moore found a hacksaw and, after some diligent work I was cut loose. He also dug up some old clothes for me, so at least I didn't have to check into the Royal York wearing nothing but a topcoat. They'd have thought I was nuts!"

Wharram's Career Ends in Heart Attack

FROM 1962–63 through 1968–69, Ken Wharram, a fleet right winger, never scored fewer than 20 goals a year with the Blackhawks. In 1968–69 he completed his 11th full season in Chicago, having compiled 30 goals and 69 points. His great speed and a deft scoring touch had netted him 252 career goals and he fully expected there'd be many more to come.

When he left his home in North Bay, Ontario, for training camp in September 1969, Wharram felt certain the Blackhawks — who'd finished in the East Division basement a few months earlier — would be vastly improved. (He would be proven right; the Hawks jumped all the way from sixth place to first that season). What he didn't know, and couldn't have foreseen, was that he would play no role in the improved fortunes of his hockey team.

During his pre–training camp physical, the team doctors detected a problem with Wharram's heart. He was hospitalized for treatment of a condition known as pericarditis — inflammation of the sac surrounding the heart — and while being treated he suffered a heart attack. Wharram made a slow recovery, thankful to be alive but despondent over the loss of his career.

The season before, he'd said something prophetic to a reporter: "You play and play and play and you never know when you won't be playing any more. Players don't like to think about it, but as your career gets longer you can't help but realize the time will come when your team doesn't want you any more, that you can't keep up any more. You see old friends fall by the wayside and you pretend it can't happen to you. But you know it can."

Chicago coach Billy Reay said of Wharram, "That the little guy's heart should be the cause of his trouble is really ironic.

Nobody in hockey has a bigger or tougher heart than Ken. He's a great man. You never had to worry about him, because as long as he had anything to give he gave it. You never had to ask."

Hawks Haunted by '67 Failure

SOME of the Blackhawks alumni, men like Hull, Mikita, Hall, and Esposito, still shake their heads in disbelief when they are reminded of a fateful afternoon at Chicago Stadium more than three decades ago.

It was the turning point in a semifinal series between the Hawks and the Toronto Maple Leafs, when the upstart Leafs robbed the Hawks and their fans of a Stanley Cup.

"There's no doubt that Toronto stole the Cup from us that year," declares club president Bill Wirtz. "We had the best team in hockey but they got the Cup."

You can't argue with Wirtz. Chicago finished the regular season in first place, 17 points ahead of Montreal and 19 points ahead of third-place Toronto, their opponents in the first playoff round. Stan Mikita and Bobby Hull were one-two in the individual scoring race, Ken Wharram was fourth, Phil Esposito seventh, and Doug Mohns ninth. Dennis Hull, with 25 goals, outscored all the Leafs, who failed to place a shooter among the top ten scorers.

Bob Pulford, now a Blackhawk front-office institution, was a member of the blue-and-white brigade that season. He remembers Leaf goalie Terry Sawchuk's performance in game five at the Stadium as "the greatest display of goaltending I ever saw. No one could have been better than Sawchuk was in that game against the Hawks."

Toronto was completely outplayed — except in goal — and outshot 49–31. Sawchuk didn't even enter the game until the second period. By then, starter Johnny Bower confessed he was "a little shaky" and coach Punch Imlach took him out.

Sawchuk, a gaunt, emotionally troubled athlete, stood in goal and faced the hard-shooting Hawks. Bobby Hull knocked him flat with his first shot, a rising slapper that practically tore Sawchuk's shoulder from his body. From the broadcast booth, we waited and watched and talked, wondering if Imlach would be forced to send Bower back into the shooting gallery. Several more minutes passed before the veteran could stagger to his feet, gingerly flexing his arm and shoulder.

He told Imlach he wanted to carry on. Then he went back to work and challenged the Hawks to knock him down again. They couldn't.

When the Leafs skated off with a 4–2 victory that afternoon it was apparent the series was all but over. A home-ice victory in game six sent Imlach and the Leafs up against Montreal for the Cup.

In the finals, the tandem of Bower and Sawchuk was fabulous in goal. Pulford played a major role, too, sending the Leafs in front, two games to one, by scoring a dramatic goal in the second overtime period of game three. The Leafs captured the Cup in six games — a championship that many say rightfully belonged to Chicago.

Hell, any old-time Chicagoan who was there will tell you that.

Close,
But No Championships

The Goalie Who Did Everything Wrong

"**H**E looks like hell in goal. The guy does everything wrong. He gives us shooters all kinds of openings and he doesn't play the angles very well. Heck, he doesn't even keep his legs together, giving you big holes to shoot at. But when you shoot at them, they're gone. He closes them up. He's amazingly quick. And the thing is, he gets the job done."

That's Bobby Orr, talking about Chicago goaltender Tony Esposito.

"Tony O's" route to NHL stardom was as unlikely as his goal-tending technique. Instead of playing Junior hockey, he went to an American college. And even though he'd led his Michigan Tech Spartans to the national championship in 1965, winning All-American honors along the way, Esposito was considered a long shot to make a career for himself as professional.

After earning his degree, the 24-year-old Esposito signed with the Montreal Canadiens, who happened to have an abundance of goalies in their system. In 1967–68 Esposito played a season for the Vancouver Canucks in the Western league, after which he was moved to Houston of the Central league. He was called up to the Canadiens for the second half of the 1968–69 season, and played in 13 games (5 wins, 4 losses, and 4 ties), collecting a pair of shutouts. But the Habs coaching staff gave no indication they liked him or approved of his unorthodox style between the pipes.

"The coach, Claude Ruel, was always barking at me if I let in a bad goal. I didn't need that, I needed support and encourage-ment," Esposito recalls. "I didn't get it in Montreal. I was glad when they let me go."

The Habs failed to protect Esposito in the 1969 intra-league draft and the Blackhawks snapped him up.

At the time, Tommy Ivan and Billy Reay thought their new goaltender would make an ideal backup to Denis DeJordy. But from the very beginning, Esposito played so well they decided to trade DeJordy and make the rookie their number-one netminder.

"We thought Tony might be pretty good someday," Billy Reay said. "But he fooled us all. It turned out he was already one of the best in the game."

Tony made a spectacular NHL debut, setting a modern-day record with 15 shutouts in 63 games. His goals-against average was 2.17 and he skated off with two major awards at season's end — the Vezina Trophy for best goaltender and the Calder for rookie of the year.

For the next fifteen seasons he was regarded as one of the pre-mier goalies in hockey. He played in 886 games, winning 423, and was selected for six All-Star games.

When he retired after the 1983–84 season, his 423 victories trailed only Terry Sawchuk's 447 and Jacques Plante's 434, and his 76 shutouts ranked seventh in NHL history.

Esposito was inducted into the Hockey Hall of Fame in 1988. The Hawks also honored him by retiring his number, 35.

Mikita Makes a
Career Change —
In the Penalty Box

D URING his first seven seasons in the NHL, Stan Mikita carried a stick in his hands and a chip on his shoulder. His willingness to flay any opponent who annoyed him saw him banished to the rinkside penalty box an average of 106 minutes per season — which is not where a team likes to station its leading scorer.

Chippiness had long been a Mikita trademark. "I had to look out for myself as a kid," he says. "When I came over from Czechoslovakia to live with relatives in St. Catharines, I got the DP (displaced person) treatment from the other kids. I didn't speak English but I knew some of the remarks thrown at me were nasty. Naturally, I retaliated and it carried over to the hockey rink. I didn't take any guff from anyone, even the referees, which cost me a few misconduct penalties over the years."

Let's go back to the night of November 6, 1966, and a game between the Blackhawks and the Boston Bruins. While sweating out a third-period retaliation penalty — the Hawks were leading 3–2 — Mikita came to the sudden realization he was doing things all wrong. It was stupid for him to be sitting in the damn penalty box. His place was on the ice.

At that moment he decided that in future he would control his temper. Instead of retaliating when fouled, he would adopt a wait-and-see attitude. Sooner or later, the opponent who nailed him would be scooting along with his head down or looking back for a pass — and Mikita would crunch him with a shoulder and drop him to the ice, gasping for breath. The best part was, it was all perfectly legal. When he'd served his time that night, a wiser Stan Mikita stepped back on the ice. "I'd just made the most important decision of my hockey life," he says.

After totaling almost six hours in penalties in the previous three seasons, he served a mere 12 minutes in 1966–67. At season's end he captured his third scoring crown in four seasons and added the Hart Trophy as most valuable player and the Lady Byng Trophy as the player judged to have shown the ideal combination of sportsmanship and gentlemanly conduct.

To prove his good behavior was not a fluke or an aberration, he came back the following season to win all three trophies again — something that had never been done by any other player.

Does Mikita remember a time when his newfound philosophy paid off?

"Oh, yes. I got even with old Gordie Howe one night. A couple of months earlier he'd reefed me with one of those iron elbows of his and knocked me flat on my ass. This night in Detroit the big lug was circling his net and having trouble handling the bouncing puck. I saw his head go down so I moved in fast and caught him with a shoulder. He staggered and fell. It felt really good at the time, but I saw him staring at me when he left the ice and I knew he was doing what I'd learned to do — take a guy's number and wait for another day to deliver some payback."

On December 15, 1999, Stan Mikita almost died after suffering an aneurysm. Surgeons placed a clamp around an artery in his brain to prevent it from bursting. Dr. Robert Beatty, a neurosurgeon and close friend of Mikita's, told reporters, "This sort of thing can be a disaster. When (brain arteries) rupture, about one-third of people die. Stan's was very thin-walled, and it was just a matter of time before it would have broken."

Mikita has recovered and returned to a fairly normal routine — and the golf course.

One of the Greatest
Games Ever Played

J OHN Ferguson, Montreal's long-retired tough guy, calls his final game in the NHL "one of the greatest games ever played." He's talking about May 18, 1971 — the seventh game of the 1971 Stanley Cup finals, played at the steamy Chicago Stadium.

That season, the Canadiens (who had missed the playoffs the year before) had a rookie coach (Al MacNeil), a rookie goalie (Ken Dryden), and a couple of players (Jean Beliveau and Frank Mahovlich) who were said to be over the hill. But Dryden's play — especially in the first round against the Boston Bruins — had been sensational. The Habs went on to oust the Minnesota North Stars in a surprisingly tough series, four games to two. The only roadblock left standing in their way to a seventeenth Stanley Cup was Billy Reay's Chicago Blackhawks.

The Hawks had steamrolled through their first season in the West Division, placing nine players on the West's All-Star Team. They finished 20 points ahead of runner-up St. Louis and they were the only team in the division to top 100 points, finishing with 107 — 10 more than Montreal, who'd placed third in the East. Bobby Hull, with 44 goals and 96 points, was fifth in league scoring, and tops among players who didn't play for Boston — the Bruins' Phil Esposito, Bobby Orr, Johnny Bucyk, and Ken Hodge took the top four slots. Bobby's brother Dennis had potted 40 goals while Stan Mikita, Pit Martin, Cliff Koroll, and Jim Pappin had been major contributors to the team's devastating attack.

In the playoffs, Bobby Hull banged in six goals in the opening round, almost single-handedly tossing the Philadelphia Flyers aside in four games. Hull and the Hawks followed up with a seven-game elimination of the New York Rangers. A victory in the final series against the Canadiens would bring the Stanley Cup back to Chicago for the first time since 1961.

The Habs' John Ferguson, who played that spring despite broken ribs suffered in an early playoff game, recalls the unhappiness, the turmoil, and the dissension in the Montreal camp as his team prepared for the final series.

"Despite all the friction, and the fact I was hurting like a son of a bitch, I figured another classic was in the works," he said.

Al MacNeil's coaching style had been severely criticized in the media, by the players (Ferguson included), and by the fans. In one game during the season, MacNeil had thrown out twenty-three different line combinations, causing uncertainty and anger among his troops. The French media lashed out at MacNeil for another reason — he had never learned the French language.

Ferguson's promise of classic hockey would prove accurate. Jim Pappin's goal gave the Hawks a 2–1 opening-game victory at the Stadium, and they came right back with a 5–3 victory in game two. In the third game, at the Montreal Forum, the Hawks jumped to a 2–0 lead, but Tony Esposito gave up goals to Peter and Frank Mahovlich and the score was tied. Yvan Cournoyer snapped a shot past Esposito early in the third and Frank Mahovlich scored his second of the game to give Montreal a 4–2 win.

John Ferguson set the tone with some big hits in game four, despite playing with a torn hip muscle that required freezing three times during the game. The Habs tied the series with a 5–2 triumph.

On home ice, the Hawks closed ranks and shut down the Habs 2–0 in game five. Henri Richard was in the penalty box when Dennis Hull slipped away for what proved to be the winning goal. Richard was used sparingly after that. At this point he and the other veterans on the team fumed over MacNeil's dizzying array of line combinations, and Richard blistered his coach after the match, telling newsmen, "I've never played for a worse coach." He would later mumble an apology.

If the Hawks thought the name-calling in the Montreal dressing room would be to their advantage in game six, they were wrong. They were leading 3–2 on Jim Pappin's go-ahead goal when the Big M struck early in the third, raising the Forum roof with the tying score. Minutes later, his brother Pete beat Esposito and the Habs nursed their 4–3 lead to the finish. Series tied at three games apiece.

CBS Television was at Chicago Stadium to bring the deciding game into millions of American homes. The Stadium ice was slow and slushy. The Hawks started fast, with Stan Mikita, Eric Nesterenko, and Keith Magnuson throwing hot shots at Dryden, who stopped them all. Late in the period, with Rejean Houle in the penalty box, Pappin was stopped close in. So was Bobby Hull. Finally, at 19:12, Dennis Hull blasted the puck in off Dryden's shoulder to give Chicago a 1–0 lead.

The Hawks went up 2–0 at 7:33 of the second period when Danny O'Shea fired a 25-footer past Dryden. Then Montreal got a break. Jacques Lemaire fired a long shot from outside the Chicago blue line — and Esposito missed it. Fans howled in disbelief when the red light flashed. Late in the period, Lemaire centered it to Henri Richard and the 35-year-old whipped the puck past Esposito. Game tied, 2–2.

Ferguson was on a shift early in the third period when Richard scored again to give Montreal a 3–2 lead. Richard dashed around Magnuson inside the blue line, skated in on Esposito, and faked him to the ice. Then he flipped the puck into the upper corner of the net.

Magnuson suffered from the humiliation of that moment for months. "I cried over it," he said. "I wanted to quit hockey, to quit everything. I wanted to move far away from Chicago, all because of Richard beating me. At least I should have tripped the guy as he went by."

The Hawks almost tied the score. With half a period to play, Jim Pappin got the puck on the lip of the crease with a gaping net in front of him. He shot and raised his arms to celebrate the goal. But Dryden's right leg shot out and deflected the puck. Nobody in the building that night, or watching on TV, could believe he made that save. You can still see it on hockey highlight tapes.

It was the Hawks' last chance. Montreal won 3–2 and left town that night with the Cup on the plane with them. And John Ferguson, who'd been on five Cup winners in eight years, was telling his mates, "That's it for me, boys. I'm through with hockey. But of all my Cups, this one over Chicago was the most satisfying."

Hawks Had Great Defensive Duos

GREAT defense pairs used to be quite common in the NHL. The Montreal Canadiens intimidated opposing forwards with the pairing of Doug Harvey and Tom Johnson. The early Boston Bruins teamed Eddie Shore with Lionel Hitchman. Later it was Shore and Babe Siebert. In the '70s Boston's Bobby Orr and Dallas Smith kept the league's best shooters at bay.

The Blackhawks also boasted some remarkable tandems. Remember Bill White and Pat Stapleton? They were as good a duo as you could find. Stapleton, the little ice general, organized sorties out of the Chicago zone, while the lean and lanky White, with arms like an octopus, wrapped up any trespassers coming the other way.

"They were the best pair I ever saw," Dennis Hull, their former teammate, states. "Pat was one of the best playmakers in the game and Bill was a master of defensive play. They worked perfectly together."

Equally effective, even though they were complete opposites, was the matchup of Pierre Pilote and Elmer Vasko. Vasko was a six-foot three-inch, 220-pound behemoth in an era when few NHLers were listed at six feet or more. While his size caused many a player to change direction and seek another route to Glenn Hall in the Chicago net, Vasko was neither a bruiser nor a goon. He took no satisfaction from hurting anyone. His steady, solid play earned him a pair of All-Star nominations.

His partner, Pierre Pilote, was half his size and had twice the number of slick moves. He handled the puck like a centerman and made heads-up plays that often led to Blackhawk goals.

Pilote was not a flamboyant type but his skills were seldom overlooked. He captured the Norris Trophy three times (1963, '64, and '65) and he was a member of eight All-Star teams. He displayed some of his best hockey in Chicago's run to the Stanley Cup in 1961.

Hull Fights Ferguson

FANS were shocked when the gloves came off and fists began to fly. The 1960s battle was between Montreal tough guy John Ferguson and Chicago's Golden Jet, Bobby Hull. It was shocking because at the time Hull was nursing a broken jaw and was wearing a helmet with a wire cage to protect the injury. Who in the world of hockey would be mean enough to punch a fellow in such a predicament? Fergie would — and did.

"Remember, whenever Montreal played Chicago in those days," he says, "the game was usually a blood battle — with a lot at stake. While most of us in the league gave Hull a lot of respect, and he certainly showed great courage in playing with his jaw wired up, I was one of his critics. In the '60s, Bobby had the big shot but I felt he didn't know the meaning of backchecking or defensive play. Toe Blake used to tell us to take the puck deep on him because he didn't like to come back. He was a super player but he knew how to lose.

"Our confrontation that night happened from a scramble," Fergie says in his book *Thunder and Lightning*. "I grabbed Hull and forced him to his knees. I was bringing my fist up, ready to deliver a haymaker, when I saw the wires in his teeth actually sparkling from the reflection of the overhead lights. I said to myself, 'John, if you throw this punch, you'll be considered the biggest rat in hockey.' I held back and didn't hit him but some people thought I did. And I was blasted in the press for it.

"Frankly, I didn't think he deserved preferential treatment while wearing the helmet and cage any more than I did when I came out of hospital and put one on for a couple of periods in a game one night. I couldn't stand wearing the thing and threw it away. Then I had two fights in the third period."

Hull Joins the WHA

ON June 27, 1972, Bobby Hull found himself riding through the streets of St. Paul, Minnesota, in a Rolls-Royce. He was there to sign a much-publicized contract with the fledgling World Hockey Association.

The Golden Jet had been demanding $250,000 a year from the Chicago Blackhawks — an amount of money the Hawks were reluctant to part with. Meanwhile his agent said, "Bobby, these guys in the WHA are bugging me every day. They really want you. What are you going to do?"

Hull said, "Listen, get them off my back, will you? Tell them I want a million up front and $250,000 a year for five years. That'll shut them up."

Well, it didn't. Bobby's agent phoned back the next day and said, "I can't believe it. They're going to meet your demands. You better grab it."

Much as Hull might have enjoyed playing in Chicago, the offer was too good to refuse. For tax purposes, Hull signed for the million-dollar bonus in St. Paul, Minnesota. After that, the Rolls whisked Hull to the airport, where he, his family, and a number of WHA owners and officials took a chartered flight to Winnipeg. There, a second ceremony took place before a huge throng at the corner of Portage and Main, Winnipeg's busiest intersection.

Hull signed with a flourish as thousands of fans cheered, and the Golden Jet flashed them his famous grin. Afterward, he spoke into a hundred microphones and tape recorders and honored a thousand requests for his autograph.

"Our league gained instant respect that day," said one of the WHA owners. "If the Blackhawks and the NHL had enticed Hull back into the fold, as a league we were doomed. We might as well have cut our throats. Hull gave us the credibility we needed desperately to be successful."

The new league's seduction of Hull had begun months earlier, in Vancouver. Learning that Hull's contract with the NHL Blackhawks was up for renewal, the WHA moguls threw his name into a hat. The lucky owner who drew it from the chapeau was Ben Hatskin of the Winnipeg Jets. Hatskin met with Hull in Vancouver and offered him a million for five years to switch leagues.

Hull's agent Harvey Wineberg said, "Not enough. Ben, come back with your very best offer." By February 1972, Hatskin, after his fellow owners had promised to chip in a hundred grand each to sweeten the pot, had raised the stakes to $2 million.

"Now you're talking, Ben," said Wineberg. "And Bobby's listening."

Blackhawk bosses Arthur and Bill Wirtz, watching from the sidelines, did little to disrupt the pending nuptials between the Golden Jet and the upstart league. They, like NHL president Clarence Campbell, foresaw an early demise of the WHA. And the Wirtzes claimed they had made a generous offer to Hull — early in the 1971–72 season, hadn't they made reference to a million-dollar pact for their star player, over five years? So what if they hadn't shown him the money — what's the hurry?

When the season was over, the Hawk front office remained strangely silent. Finally, the team unveiled its five-year, million-dollar offer. "But we can't match the Winnipeg offer," Bill Wirtz cautioned. By then, Hull was enamored of the WHA and the Jets' proposal. In Winnipeg, he could just play, or he could add coaching duties to his portfolio if he wished, and at the end of the five years he had a chance to stay on as a team executive at $100,000 per annum. In effect, the Chicago bid to keep him came far too late, and was for much too little. What's more, Hull was stung by the Blackhawks' attitude toward him. They didn't seem to care!

"Chicago must have thought I was bluffing about leaving," Hull said on that June day in Winnipeg. "I probably would have stayed in Chicago if the Wirtz family had made me a decent offer. And come up with it earlier. I mean, I told them I didn't want to leave. Who in his right mind wants to pick up and move his family to a new city and a new league after fifteen years in the NHL? But they didn't appear to even want to sit down and talk with me."

The Golden Jet shook his head and added, "You can say that I have no regrets about leaving Chicago. None at all."

Those of us who know him didn't believe him. He must have harbored a few regrets. Don Cherry says, "I know Bobby and if you could crawl in his heart, I'm sure he'd say, 'I should never have left Chicago.' He was the most popular guy in the entire city. He would have played a lot longer and he would have been a lot happier."

Dennis Hull says, "Bobby left and that was devastating to the rest of the team. In fact, Jim Pappin talked to the players and convinced us we should offer to give up some of our salaries if it meant we could keep Bobby, who was the mainstay of our team. We were naîve to think the Hawks didn't have enough money to satisfy Bobby. So we agreed to Pappin's proposal. But it was too late."

Hawks Vote to Strike

C AN you believe the Blackhawks once voted to go on strike — in the middle of the Stanley Cup playoffs?

It happened in the spring of 1972. And all because of a few curved hockey sticks.

In the opening round of the playoffs, the Hawks disposed of the Pittsburgh Penguins in four games. But in game two of the series, Dennis Hull had his stick confiscated by the referee with about a minute to play. He was told the stick was illegal. Hull was later fined $500 (as was the club) when the curvature in the blade of his stick was found to be three-eighths of an inch over the legal limit of half an inch.

NHL president Clarence Campbell, a spectator at the game, charged Hull with "tampering" with the stick and used the word "cheating" to describe Hull's action.

After the game, outside the Hawks' dressing room in the bowels of the cavernous Chicago Stadium, Campbell was accosted by general manager Tommy Ivan, whose face was red with rage.

"Mr. Campbell, sticks are supposed to be checked before each game by one of your supervisors. That was one of your own directives. Hull's stick was checked and approved. There's nothing that says there can be an appeal by either team."

Campbell maintained that Hull had tampered with the stick after it had been given a stamp of approval by playoff supervisor Dutch Van Deelen. "And that's breaking the rules."

Dennis Hull denied the accusation. "I did nothing to that stick after it was stamped," he said. "It's an idiotic rule anyway. It's stupid. They can keep fining me until I'm broke. Then I'll go home."

Brother Bobby supported Dennis, saying the rule was ludicrous. "The rule must have been made by someone who doesn't know hockey," he said. "Making a guy change his stick in mid-career is like asking a carpenter to work with dull tools."

The next day, a surprise visitor charged into the Chicago camp. Alan Eagleson, head of the NHL Players Association, had flown in from Toronto and after huddling with the disgruntled Hawks for an hour, he came out shooting with both barrels blazing.

"The NHL has no right whatsoever to enact the stick rule without consulting the players," he told reporters. "The league is going to learn that the players should and will have some voice in the way the game is run. The Chicago players have met and voted to strike."

Strike! A lot of mouths popped open when that word was used.

The vote to strike and to refuse to take part in the rest of the playoffs was unanimous, reporters were told. But there was a condition, Eagleson explained: the strike was contingent on the other teams involved in the playoffs lending their support with a similar strike vote.

You can imagine the feedback Eagleson and the Hawks players got from the members of the other teams. "You guys crazy? Give up our chance for some real playoff money because Dennis Hull uses an illegal stick? Get real. Call us back when a really important issue comes along."

Somewhat embarrassed, the Hawks decided not to strike after all.

As usual, Clarence Campbell got the last word: "Contributing a voice to NHL rules is none of the players' business," he said. "I'm surprised that Alan Eagleson would be a party to [a strike vote]." He added: "Bobby Hull is employing this as a tactic to help tear apart the Players Association. He's been against the Association since it failed to back him in a personal matter a few years ago." He was referring to the Golden Jet's twelve-game holdout in 1969 when he had contract problems with Chicago management.

Bobby Hull could only shake his head over the president's statement and say, "Gee, I don't know why Mr. Campbell is so mad at me."

The Atomic Redhead

A T 32 years of age, his body bruised and battered, his right knee having been opened three times by a surgeon's scalpel, the Atomic Redhead was forced to retire. The Atomic Redhead was one of the most popular of all the Blackhawks: team captain Keith Magnuson.

Chicago hockey writer Bob Verdi gave Magnuson his nickname and wrote fondly of him in *The Hockey News* when Maggie quit the game in November 1979.

From the first time he came bursting through the chute in 1969 — one of several rookies who would lead the Blackhawks from last place to first — the Atomic Redhead never stopped trying, Verdi wrote.

"I wasn't helping anymore," Maggie said. "I knew I couldn't play every game because the knee wasn't getting any better. I knew that even when I played, I couldn't do what I wanted to.

"I didn't have much ability to begin with. I couldn't skate that well, or shoot that well, or pass the puck that well. I always had to labor, even when everything was going all right. So when it wasn't going all right . . ."

Someone once said that if Magnuson's body were a bank account, it long ago would have been overdrawn. He broke so many bones for the Blackhawks, and sipped so many portions of liquid slop through fractured jaws, and tiptoed through so many summers with casts and canes and assorted pains. He said he would break his neck for his team, and a couple of times he even came close to doing that.

Numbers will not send him to the Hall of Fame. He collected 17 goals in 657 regular season and playoff games. He was quite capable defensively, and quite beatable in pugilistic encounters. For every Earl Heiskala or Gene Carr who was his victim, Magnuson was on the canvas tenfold. But he just kept on truckin' because it only hurt for a little while.

"His value never showed up in the stats," said Eddie Johnston, the Blackhawks' vibrant new coach whom Magnuson will now assist. "He had heart. When he played, when he practiced, he always had spirit. I wish I could spread it around to some of these other guys."

Magnuson amassed a remarkable number of penalty minutes — 1,606 — but he always dropped his stick and hit you from up front. When Bugsy Watson whacked him with a questionable shot some years back, Magnuson, his jaw unhinged again, might have sought revenge. But he didn't. You live by the sword, you die by the sword. And anyway, Magnuson probably realized that Watson was a mirror image of himself: *enfant terrible* on ice, solid community asset off ice.

His charisma and personality and care for his fellow man have taken him far. If Magnuson were a baseball or football player he might have been on more magazine covers and reaped more endorsements. But because hockey in general and the Blackhawks in particular are either unwilling or unable to portray their athletes as people, Magnuson and his ilk exist in relative obscurity.

But that doesn't bother him. What bothers him is that he didn't trip Henri Richard before the Pocket Rocket scored the winning goal in game seven of a palpitating 1971 Stanley Cup final. What Magnuson should realize is that when Richard started his engines, there was no stopping him.

However, Magnuson need not apologize for ever going to the pay window. He didn't have much talent, true. Then again, maybe the greatest talent of all is the talent to work.

Wildest Game in Chicago History

ON the final day of the 1969–70 NHL season, the Chicago Blackhawks faced the Montreal Canadiens at Chicago Stadium in a match that has often been called "the wildest game in NHL history."

Can you believe the Canadiens considered starting the game without a goaltender? It's true — but I'm getting ahead of the story.

Going into the final day's action, Chicago and Boston were tied for first place in the East Division with 97 points. The Hawks had 44 wins to the Bruins' 39, so if the teams finished the season tied in points, first place would go to Chicago. Detroit, with 95 points, could only finish third. The battle for fourth place, and the final playoff spot, was also down to the wire — Montreal held a two-point advantage (92–90) over the New York Rangers.

The Hawks badly wanted to finish first because they'd finished in the East Division basement the year before. Not since the 1930s had a team roared from last place one season to first the next. During their game with the Habs, the Hawks would keep a watchful eye on the out-of-town scoreboard. Boston was playing Toronto, and a Bruin victory would put Chicago into a must-win situation.

As the game began, the Habs already knew they were in desperate straits. The Rangers had played that afternoon, walloping Detroit 9–5, and earning two points that put them into a tie with Montreal at 92. The clubs were now also tied in wins, with 38 apiece.

The Habs needed a win or a tie to be sure of securing fourth place. But, if they lost to Chicago, there was still a chance — albeit a slim one — of making the playoffs. Under league rules, fourth place would go to the team that had scored the most goals. The Rangers' outburst against the Wings had given them an edge in that category, 246–242. So if the Canadiens lost, they could still make the playoffs, as long as they scored at least five goals against the Blackhawks. Get it?

Anyway, that's why Montreal coach Claude Ruel gave serious thought to starting the game at the Stadium with six skaters and no netminder. The way he saw it, the Hawks would open up a big lead shooting into the empty net, then Chicago's top players would be given a rest and Ruel's Habs might score the five goals they needed against rookie goalie Tony Esposito.

As game time neared, Ruel decided against the unorthodox move. He realized he would be handing first place to the Hawks, which would be most unfair to Boston.

For Ruel to ask his players to score five times against Tony Esposito was asking a lot, but the margin might have been even greater. In the afternoon contest, New York had pulled goalie Ed Giacomin late in the game in an effort to add to their 9–3 lead. The Red Wings then responded with a pair of empty-net goals.·

As the Chicago–Montreal game got under way, it quickly became apparent that Boston would win their game against the

Maple Leafs. The Hawks knew the onus was on them to win. They took a 3–2 lead into the third period on goals from Jim Pappin, Pit Martin, and Bobby Hull. Suddenly Martin scored two more goals, putting the game virtually out of Montreal's reach.

Behind the Habs bench, Ruel's priority became goals, not points. He needed three more — and in a hurry. With nine minutes left on the clock, Ruel stunned the Stadium crowd by yanking goalie Rogie Vachon and putting out an extra skater.

Under extreme pressure to score, the Habs faltered badly, failing to get one decent shot on Esposito in almost half a period of hockey.

The Hawks, meanwhile, calmly potted goal after goal into the gaping net. The fans whooped it up when Eric Nesterenko, Cliff Koroll, Bobby Hull, Dennis Hull, and Gerry Pinder all found the inviting target. At the final buzzer, the score was 10–2. The Canadiens skated off in a daze, their playoff hopes dashed.

Such a strange ending to a season can never happen again. The rules were changed shortly thereafter to make goals scored a virtually irrelevant factor to the order of finish in the NHL standings.

The game was memorable for several reasons: the incredible Chicago spree of five empty-net goals in a nine-minute span; their amazing recovery from worst to first in the space of one year; and, for the first time, there was no Canadian team in the Stanley Cup playoffs.

You may wonder how the Blackhawks, with 99 points, fared in the 1970 playoffs. In the first round, they ousted Detroit in four straight games — and by the same score each time, 4–2. They ran into real grief against the Bruins and were swept in four straight. The Bruins went on to meet St. Louis in the finals and eliminated the expansion team in four games. The Bruins of Orr, Esposito, and Cheevers captured the Stanley Cup in a mere 14 playoff games.

Bill Wirtz Meets the Duke

AT the 1991 All-Star weekend in Chicago, Mike Keenan, then coach of the Blackhawks, chuckled as he told me a story about his boss, Bill Wirtz.

Mr. Wirtz, among other things, owned the Bismarck Hotel in Chicago. From time to time, he would make use of the penthouse suite in the hotel. One night, years ago, he comes home from a business trip. He's tuckered out and decides to stay at the hotel. When he opens the door to his suite, he sees a stranger, a bald-headed man sitting on the bed and taking a long swallow from a bottle of booze.

Wirtz enters the room, slams the door behind him and says angrily, "Who the hell are you, pal? And what the hell are you doing in my suite?

The stranger snarls back. "Your suite? This is my suite. The manager gave it to me. Say, who the hell are you to barge in on me like this?"

"Who am I?" Wirtz roars. "I'm the owner of this hotel. Say, what the hell's your name?"

The guy says, "I'm John Wayne, the movie actor."

This obvious lie infuriates Wirtz. He grabs the stranger by the shirt and pushes him back on the bed. "Like hell you're John Wayne, you bald-headed old bugger," he says, shaking the stranger until his teeth begin to rattle. "I'd know John Wayne if I saw him. And you're not him."

Now the two big men begin wrestling around on the bed until the stranger yells, "Wait a minute, wait a minute!" He reaches for a toupee on the nightstand and slaps it on his head. "Now do you believe it's me?" he shouts.

Wirtz lets go of the man's shirt and stares at him. He starts to laugh. "Yeah, now I believe you, John." He grabs Wayne's big hand and pumps it. Then he slaps him on the back. "Hey, Duke," he says. "Welcome to Chicago."

Tommy Ivan Passes

TOMMY Ivan was a centerman in his playing days. Not quite NHL caliber, but a clever playmaker who could skate. At age 27, a fractured cheekbone put him on the shelf. That's when he decided to explore other avenues in the game. He eventually caught on with the Detroit Red Wing organization as a scout, then as a coach.

In 1945–46, in Omaha, he became Gordie Howe's first pro coach. The next year, he moved up to Indianapolis of the American Hockey League. And a year later he became head coach in Detroit, where he established a remarkable record. His Red Wings finished in first place in the NHL standings for six consecutive seasons and they won the Stanley Cup three times. Ivan must have thought the coaching profession was a piece of cake.

Why then did he leave Detroit for a Chicago franchise that played a crude form of unsuccessful hockey, a team that had just turned in an odious record of 12-51-7?

"It was the challenge more than anything," he once said. "I liked Detroit, but in Chicago I had a new title — general manager. I liked that, too."

Owners Jim Norris and Arthur Wirtz gave Ivan a hefty budget, hoping he'd use it to acquire some good players. But talent was scarce, so Ivan pumped the money into player development. Eventually the investment paid off and the talent arrived: Bobby and Dennis Hull, Chico Maki, Stan Mikita, Elmer Vasko, and Pierre Pilote.

And the crowds arrived, too. Ivan remembered when as few as 3,000 fans turned out for Blackhawk games. By the 1960–61 season the old Stadium was jammed whenever Hull and Company entertained. And in the spring of 1961, when the third-place club played inspired hockey in the playoffs and captured the Stanley Cup, their first since 1938, Ivan took great pride in the accomplishment.

At only 5'5" and 150 pounds, Harold "Mush" March played 17 years with the Hawks, beginning in 1928–29. He tallied a career-high 37 points in his 16th season before a knee injury forced him to retire.

"Mush" March

Earl Seibert was a first- or second-team All-Star for 10 of his 15 seasons in the NHL. Sadly, his death in 1990 went virtually unnoticed by the hockey world.

EARL SEIBERT
CHICAGO "BLACK HAWKS"—Defence
LITHOGRAPHED IN CANADA

TOP LEFT: Born in Odessa, Russia, John Gottselig led the Hawks to their first two Stanley Cups, in 1934 and 1938. Later he became a coach, public relations director, and assistant to the club president.
— Public Archives of Canada

TOP RIGHT: Minnesota native Mike Karakas was the rookie of the year in 1936, and two years later sparked the Hawks to a surprise Stanley Cup victory.
— Public Archives of Canada

RIGHT: Doug Bentley was a key member of Chicago's famed Pony Line, with his brother Max and Bill Mosienko. Doug led the NHL in scoring in 1943.
— Chas. S. Gekler

Defenseman Bob Goldham
joined the Hawks in 1947.
He was one of five Leafs
acquired for all-star center
Max Bentley.

In this photo, Max Bentley,
traded to Toronto in 1947
after winning two scoring
titles with the Hawks,
tries to put the puck past
goaltender Harry Lumley.

— Michael Burns

Orchestra leader Sammy Kaye (center) is flanked by Chicago coach Charlie Conacher (far left), Roy Conacher, Doug Bentley, and Gus Bodnar.
— Jerry Saltsberg & Associates

Coach Charlie Conacher gathers his players for a pep talk during the 1947–48 season. In the attentive group are brother Roy, Bob Goldham, John Mariucci, Emile Francis, Doug Bentley, Bud Poile, Gus Bodnar, and Bill Gadsby. — Turofsky/Hockey Hall of Fame

Hawk stars of the 1950s included Gus Bodnar (left), Al Rollins, Cal Gardner,
and Gus Mortson. Goalie Rollins won the Hart Trophy in 1954.
— Turofsky/Hockey Hall of Fame

Glenn Hall, "Mr. Goalie," set an
amazing record by playing in 502
consecutive games from 1955 to 1962.
— Hockey Hall of Fame

An unidentified Hawk goaltender
is helped to the dressing room
after sustaining an injury in a
game in the late 1940s.

Eddie Litzenberger remains the only player ever to win the Calder Trophy after being traded (from Montreal to Chicago) during his rookie season.

Glenn Hall covers up after Pierre Pilote sends Toronto's Gerry James flying in a game in the 1950s.

Eddie Litzenberger

Toronto's Marcel Pronovost (#3) and goalie Johnny Bower stymie the "Golden Jet," Bobby Hull. All three became Hall of Famers.

Three popular Hawks: Keith Magnuson (#3), Eric Nesterenko (#15), and Bobby Hull (#9). Nesterenko and Magnuson were among the first NHLers to successfully combine pro hockey and a good education.

In his post-hockey career, Dennis Hull became a popular after-dinner speaker.

Bobby Hull, who jumped to the WHA in 1972, remains the most famous Blackhawk of them all. Here he battles Montreal enforcer John Ferguson.

"It was one of my biggest thrills in hockey," he said.

Not *the* biggest?

"Well, I can't forget my Red Wing team of 1951–52 when we finished first for the fourth straight time and captured the Cup in eight straight games. It's hard to beat the thrill of a run like that."

He got another thrill in 1967, when his Hawks captured first place in the NHL standings for the first time in club history. And another when he was inducted into the Hockey Hall of Fame as a builder of the game in 1974.

Ivan was one of the first general managers to tap into U.S. talent for his team, and he was partially responsible for assembling the club of amateurs that stunned the hockey world in 1980 with a gold-medal victory at the Winter Olympics in Lake Placid, New York.

If there's one blot on Ivan's management record it's his engineering of the deal that sent Phil Esposito, Ken Hodge, and Fred Stanfield to Boston in May 1967.

Esposito recalls his brief time in Chicago fondly. "Great years. Oh, they were great years. Bobby (Hull) and I and Chico (Maki) formed a line and did we click! It was unbelievable. We started to score and we kept on going. I thought I'd be there forever."

Dennis Hull adds, "We could see that Phil was going to be a remarkable player. Bobby and Phil and Chico were becoming one of the dominant lines in the NHL. We could all see that. Why Tommy Ivan couldn't see it is beyond belief. Bobby never played with anyone of note after Phil left. He would play with whoever was left on the team. Ask people who Bobby played with after Esposito and they'll be hard pressed to tell you."

Ivan seldom spoke of the deal that has been called the most lopsided in league history. He remained the Hawks' general manager until 1977 when, at age 76, he turned the position over to Bob Pulford and accepted a less rigorous front-office role as a vice president.

He passed away in 1999 at age 88.

Pinder Pops Off

LEFT winger Gerry Pinder wasn't a Blackhawk for long — only two seasons — and he's remembered today as a player who was never shy to voice an opinion.

In his sophomore season, 1970–71, during which he scored a mere 13 goals, Pinder and the Hawks steamrolled all the way to the Stanley Cup finals, only to lose 3–2 to Ken Dryden, Henri Richard, and the rest of the Montreal Canadiens in the seventh and deciding game.

During the semifinal series against the New York Rangers, Pinder howled about his lot in life (not enough ice time) and blasted his coach, Billy Reay.

The Hawks had routed the Rangers 7–1 in game four of the series, during which Pinder was the only Hawk not to hit the ice. Afterwards the 22-year-old pilloried Reay, saying, "He shafted me and lied to me all season. He used bush-league tactics and I don't think I could ever lace up my skates for that man again."

Pinder left the team, skipping practices, team meetings, and the fifth game of the series.

Two days after his scathing comments made it into all the papers, Pinder had a change of heart. He apologized profusely to Reay, to the Blackhawks management, and to anyone else he might have offended: "I'm afraid I blew my stack. I'm sorry I said what I did. Anything I said that was detrimental to the rest of the players, the organization — and especially Billy Reay — I regret. I owe them all a sincere apology."

The Hawks immediately welcomed Pinder back into the fold and arranged for him to fly to New York for the sixth game of the series. Reay didn't give the prodigal forward any ice time but in game seven, back in Chicago, Pinder did play and was part of Chicago's 4–2 series-winning victory.

Pinder wasn't the only NHL player frustrated with his coach that spring. During the finals, Montreal's Henri Richard called his coach, Al MacNeil, "incompetent" and "the worst coach I ever played for."

The difference between Pinder's outburst and Richard's? Richard, idol of millions and holder of a record number of Stanley Cup rings, was able to lead his team to their seventeenth Stanley Cup championship by scoring the tying and winning goals. His angry words helped bring MacNeil's coaching career to a crashing end. Pinder's ill-timed blast at Reay resulted in a much different outcome. Before the next season's training camp, he was dealt to the lowly California Golden Seals. It was about as far away from Chicago Stadium as the Hawks could possibly send him.

Blackhawk Goalie Helps Montreal to Cup Win

GOALTENDER Gary (Suitcase) Smith was a big, blond, good-looking chap known as much for his eccentricity as for his netminding. He would wander up ice as far as the blue line. Rather than clear the puck with his stick, he would often drop kick it down the ice. And he would strip off all of his equipment, and casually put it on again, between periods of a game.

The well-traveled Smith played for eight different NHL teams, but his most memorable stint was with the Chicago Blackhawks, with whom he went to the Stanley Cup finals in 1973. Little did he know that a quip he made in jest before the opening game of that final series would be credited with turning the tide of the series toward Chicago's opponents, the Montreal Canadiens.

During the warmup before game one, Smith chatted briefly with Montreal's Murray Wilson. They were old friends, having grown up together in Ottawa. Smith was only needling Wilson when he said, "Murray, what are you going to do with your $10,000 share of the playoff money?"

Smith was referring to the losers' share of the playoff pot. As it turned out, his innocent joking turned out to be a fatal slip of the tongue. Standing within earshot was Henri Richard, who glared at Smith but said nothing. For the rest of the warmup Richard skated at Wilson's heels. "That Smith," he said, "you know what he was telling you, Murray? He was telling you that we will lose. He thinks he's going to get the winners' share of $15,000. He is very arrogant. He makes me very, very mad."

Then Richard stood up in the dressing room and told the rest of the Canadiens what Smith had said to Wilson. Everyone could see that the Pocket Rocket was furious and ready to wipe the smile off Smith's handsome face.

Richard, one of the greatest competitors in Stanley Cup history, owned the puck throughout the series. The Habs wiped out Chicago in six games, and Henri established a remarkable record by winning his eleventh Stanley Cup.

Wilson would later say, "I always felt my friend Gary helped us win that Cup. He should never have infuriated Henri and helped him to set a record that may last forever."

Hull Banished from Team Canada

THERE'S a little-known story behind the banishment of Bobby Hull from the Team Canada roster in 1972. It concerns a costly slip of the tongue — made by the Golden Jet himself — that cost him a chance to play in hockey's greatest series.

At the same time, if it hadn't been for Hull's boss of many years, Chicago owner Bill Wirtz, the famous Team Canada–Soviet series of 1972 — now known as the Series of the Century — might never have happened.

In the weeks leading up to the series, an event Alan Eagleson, executive director of the NHL Players Association, had been touting since 1969, there was as much drama behind the scenes as would later be displayed in the eight games on the ice. NHL president Clarence Campbell responded to Alan Eagleson's announcement that the series would be played in September 1972 by stating, "That may be, but there won't be any NHL players on the Canadian side." At that point Wirtz, a powerful voice in hockey, stepped into the controversy, supporting Eagleson and persuading his fellow owners to allow the participation of their star players. Campbell backed off, but not before insisting that all players on Team Canada be signed to NHL contracts.

That ruling protected the Team Canada roster from players who had recently jumped to the upstart World Hockey Association — including superstar Bobby Hull, who had signed with the league's Winnipeg Jets.

Chicago could have made a case for Hull by claiming he still had a signed contract with the club — even though it was clear he would battle in the courts if necessary for the right to play in the rival circuit.

Eagleson battled hard to have Hull named to the team. With fifteen fabulous NHL seasons behind him, during which he had scored 604 goals and reached 50 goals in a season five times, it was obvious he deserved a place on the roster. Head coach Harry Sinden and assistant coach John Ferguson agreed. They were certain that Hull would be a major asset and should be named to the squad.

When the Eagleson group started recruiting players, Hull's name was first on the list and he quickly agreed to play. Like all the other players invited to join the team, he was sworn to secrecy until a formal announcement of the roster could be made.

But Hull was never one to keep a secret. He loved to talk, especially over a couple of bottles of red wine. During or after a celebrity sports dinner in the Maritimes, he spoke of his invitation to join Team Canada.

When Clarence Campbell heard about Hull's statement, he

called Eagleson to protest. League governors huddled and decided that, if Hull played, the contracts of players named to the team would no longer be guaranteed by their NHL clubs in the event of injury.

This was a major blow to the Eagleson group. Team Canada was now faced with a tough choice: buy expensive insurance to guarantee contracts, or leave Bobby Hull off the team. They chose the latter and all hell broke out across Canada. Public reaction was furious. Prime Minister Trudeau spoke out for Hull and so did many parliamentarians.

"The biggest disappointment in my life was not being able to represent Canada in the famous 1972 series with the Soviet Union," Hull says today. "I knew maybe a little more than others how good the Russian players were. I remember saying at the time if the Soviets were going to challenge the NHL they had a good chance of winning. All of those reports that they couldn't skate, they couldn't pass, they had poor goaltending — I knew that was all a bunch of malarkey."

Eagleson, the NHL, and Team Canada were all blamed for Hull's expulsion, but the NHL owners sighed in relief when Hull was not included. To the governors, he was a defector and his presence on the roster would only add credibility to the rival league. They were beginning to realize it had been a huge mistake to let him get away.

What wasn't generally known at the time was that Hull himself was most responsible for his exclusion. If he hadn't opened his mouth at that sports banquet in the Maritimes, he would have been named to the squad first and the chips would have fallen later.

"Hull was the only player who broke the secrecy code we demanded," Alan Eagleson once said. "If we had been able to announce his name at our press conference as one of the team members, there's no way on earth anybody would have dared to kick him off."

Dennis Hull
Signs for Ten Years

SOMEWHERE in Manitoba, Dennis Hull and I are in the back of a limo, driving to or from another speaking engagement. We meet at several of these each year. It gives me a chance to add another few stories to my collection of Hull anecdotes. Dennis, as most folks know, is a masterful storyteller. This time I begin by asking him about signing with the Hawks at a time when the WHA was offering big contracts to NHL stars.

It was 1973, the year the WHA was signing guys. Bobby was gone to Winnipeg for a million dollars and Ralph Backstrom and Pat Stapleton were ready to jump leagues, too. So the main guys on the Blackhawks were Jim Pappin, Pit Martin, and myself. We didn't know it but management had decided to sign us until we were all forty years old. I was the youngest in the group — I'd turned 29 — so I was looking at a ten-year contract. Not bad, eh?

When I first went in to see Tommy Ivan I had no idea what he was going to offer me but I speculated. I remember thinking I'd ask him for a million dollars for the next ten years. Seemed like a good figure at the time.

Well, Tommy says to me, "I'm going to make you a one-time only offer. It's for ten years at a million and a half." Geez, I hadn't said a word and already he's willing to give me half a million more than I expected. Well, a light went on and I thought, if they're offering me that much they may be willing to pay me even more. So I said, "Tommy, I was thinking $1,750,000."

Tommy got all upset. He was incensed that I'd asked for $250,000 more. So he called Bill Wirtz in and told Mr. Wirtz I was being outrageous in my demands and wanted nothing more to do with me. Bill Wirtz said, "Calm down, Tommy, calm down. We'll settle this somehow." He turned to me and said, "Dennis, are you a gambler?"

I said, "No, I'm not a gambler."

He ignored me and pulled a quarter from his pocket and said, "Well, let's flip for the $250,000. Call it in the air." And the quarter went spinning up over his head.

I yelled, "Heads."

He caught the quarter and turned it over in his hand, shielding it from me and Tommy. He said, "Heads it is."

So that's how I got $250,000 more than I expected to get that day. I asked Bill from time to time if the quarter had really come down heads. He would say, "Of course it did. You think I give my money away?"

But he *did* give his money away. He was extremely generous. I know Doug Jarrett wanted to buy a house one year and he went to see Mr. Wirtz. Bill said, "How much do you need to buy the house?" Doug said, "About forty grand." So Bill gave him a $40,000 raise.

The tape recorder continues to run and Dennis talks about a number of subjects and people.

Let me tell you about my breakthrough season with the Hawks. It was my third season as a pro and I'd played most of 1965–66 in the minors — with St. Louis. Now a new season begins and I'm back up with the Hawks and I played in the first six games. But there was a league rule that if you played in more than six games you couldn't be sent down. Now Billy Reay says to my brother Bobby, "I think I'm going to send Dennis back to the minors for another year."

That troubled Bobby, so we're driving to the game that night and he tells me that I won't be playing, that Reay plans to keep me on the bench all night. He won't play me because if he does he'll be stuck with me for the rest of the season.

Bobby says to me, "Here's what we're going to do. You know how I start the game and usually stay out there two or three minutes? Tonight when they drop the puck I'll circle behind the net and come right near the Chicago bench. Then I'll jump off and you be ready to jump on, okay?"

I say, "Okay."

So that's what happened. Bobby whips past the bench in the first few seconds, gives me a nod and leaps over the boards. I begin to jump on but by then Billy Reay figures out what's going on and moves fast. He reaches out and grabs me by the back of the jersey just as my skates hit the ice. By then it was too late. I was already legally in the game. And it turned out well because I scored 25 goals that season.

On J.P. Bordeleau:

There was some kind of a meeting in Chicago one day and J.P. Bordeleau, one of our Rhodes Scholars on the Hawks, was asked to attend. Don't ask me why. So I told him, "J.P., be sure and keep the minutes of the meeting." He said, "Ho-kay, Dennis."

Now he comes out of the meeting and he sees me there. He calls over, "Hey, Dennis, twelve minutes."

One year Billy Reay said he was sick and tired of all the silly questions sportswriters ask after hockey games. So he decided he wasn't going to allow his players to speak to the media from then on, especially after Ranger games. He hated those New York guys. But Clarence Campbell got wind of it. He stepped in and said Billy had to make players available to the press. So Billy came up with the idea of a "designated speaker" to field questions from reporters after the games. Impishly, he selected J.P. Bordeleau to do the talking. At the time, J.P. really struggled with the English language so you can imagine what kind of answers he gave. That really ticked off the media but everyone on the team thought it was hilarious — except J.P., of course.

In 1972, J.P. was drafted by a team in the WHA — the Los Angeles Sharks. When he talked about jumping to the Sharks, I told him I'd heard the team was going to wear jerseys with a big fin stuck on the back. That must have got him thinking because I heard him tell one of the guys, "I hope that damn fin won't get in the way when I'm deking."

On Bobby leaving Chicago:

I'd been drafted by the Miami Screaming Eagles of the new league and I knew they didn't even have a rink to play in. But the name Screaming Eagles intrigued me, so I did a lot of screaming in practices. We made a lot of fun of the WHA that season. Most of us had been drafted by one team or the other but we were all amazed when we heard that Bobby was actually going to make the jump to Winnipeg.

My brother was an institution in Chicago. But you had a couple of strong-willed guys — Bill Wirtz and Bobby — who were unwilling or unable to bend. They just couldn't come together.

Bobby had said, "If someone offers me a million dollars, I'll go the WHA." And a couple of days later Winnipeg came up with the dough. Bobby was always a man of his word. He told everybody, "Look, I said I'd go for a million. Now I've got to stick with it."

Naturally, we all wanted him to stay. Jim Pappin even started a little movement among the Blackhawks. If money was the only problem, we were all willing to take a little less on our contracts just to keep Bobby in Chicago. That's something you don't often encounter in sports.

But it wasn't a money issue. It was just a matter of a couple of stubborn guys who were not willing to bend. It was a shame for our club because we were right on the brink of having a great team.

The WHA probably would never have made it through the first year if Bobby hadn't joined it. He changed the structure of hockey salaries everywhere when he went there and got all that money.

Later, his son Brett did exactly the same thing. He signed for a couple of million and suddenly all the players were asking for big money contracts.

On playing in Montreal:

We had some great times in Montreal. After Maurice Richard retired, we used to come off the ice and the Rocket sat right over the entrance where we came off the ice. And he'd shout at us. The Rocket liked to needle Stan Mikita because Stan was always getting involved with Henri Richard, the Rocket's brother. As opposing centers, they were always yapping at each other and swatting each other with their sticks.

The Rocket would sit there nursing a beer and he'd shout, "Mikita, you little DP, if I was out there I'd kill you. You touch my brudder once more, you son huv a bitch, I come out there and keel you."

So we're coming off the ice one time and Mikita says to me, "Watch this." When the Rocket gave him an earful he reached up and hit Richard's beer container with his stick, dumping beer all over the Rocket's pants.

Oh, the Rocket was mad.

A few seasons after Bobby scored his 50 goals we went to Montreal and there was the Rocket ready to greet us. This time he ignored Mikita and got on Bobby's case.

"Hey, Bo-bee, you tink you're such a big deal scoring 50 goals. I did it in 50 games."

And you know how Bobby was. He'd grin and yell back, "You're right, Rocket. That's a great feat. I'm sure you were a lot better player than I am. A lot better." He almost apologized to the Rocket for scoring 50.

So the next time we're at the Forum, the Rocket starts in again. "Hey Bo-bee!" Then he didn't seem to know what to say. So he yelled out, "Hey, Bo-bee. You know what? Someday you gonna be big and fat like me."

In '67 I was playing against the Canadiens' big line, centered by Jean Beliveau. He had Yvan Cournoyer and Gilles Tremblay as wingers. Now Beliveau breaks away from us and he goes in one-on-one against Pierre Pilote, and Pilote falls down. So I rush over at an angle and catch Beliveau. I give him a dandy two-hander right across the arm. I fucking drilled him. Now this is Beliveau, my hero growing up. I even had a big picture of him in my bedroom. Well, he shook off my check and with one hand threw the puck into the Chicago net. Then he turned to me and said, "Dennis, I did not expect that from you."

Well, I could have crawled under the Habs logo at center ice. I said, "Geez, I'm sorry, Jean. I'll never do that again."

So Billy Reay, when I go to the bench, said, "What are you doing talking to that guy? What's going on out there?"

I said, "I wanted to apologize to Jean."

He said, "Don't be talking to those guys. What do you mean apologize? You never apologize to those guys."

Sometimes with Dennis it's difficult to discern fact from fiction. Like the following:

You may not believe this story, but my brother Bobby was in Montreal one time and he met a hooker on the street. He says, "How much?"

She says, "A hundred bucks."

Bobby says, "Hell, I wouldn't give you ten bucks."

Later that day, Bobby and his wife come out of the hotel and start walking down the street. And who's coming toward them but the hooker he talked to earlier. Bobby walks right by pretending he doesn't see her when the hooker shouts back at him, "See what you get for ten bucks."

You know how coaches often say, "We're all the same on this team." Billy Reay used to tell us, "We're not all the same on this team. Bobby and Stan are a lot better than the rest of you guys. Understand?" We all understood. We accepted that.

Bobby was late for the team bus one day and the guys are all grumbling about it.

"Let's go, Billy. Let's go."

Billy Reay turns in his seat and says, "Listen, if it was one of you young guys who was late, we'd go. But it's Bobby, so we'll wait."

Now Bobby, driving a white Corvette, comes racing down the street and the car screeches to a halt beside the bus. And there's a familiar-looking woman in the car with him. Remember the Paul Newman movie *Cool Hand Luke*, and the actress who was washing her car when the chain gang walked by? What a figure! And that's the woman Bobby was with.

So Billy Reay leaps from his seat, grabs the handle on the bus door and yanks it open. He yells, "Bobby, get on this bus right now!" He pauses for a second, then shouts, "And bring her with you." So Bobby and the actress get on the bus and she parades up and down the aisle saying hello to everyone.

Billy had a great sense of humor. A wonderful man, Billy Reay.

On Pierre Pilote:

Pierre was a good man. Whenever we went to Boston Doug Jarrett and I would wind up in Pierre's room at the hotel. Why? Because we loved to hear him order that good Boston clam chowder from room service. He'd get on the phone and he always ordered three tureens of chowder. But it often came out "three latrines of chowder." It always cracked us up.

On Dale Tallon:

Another guy with a good sense of humor. One of our defensemen came roaring in from the point in New Jersey one night and bowled over Devils goaltender Chris Terreri. Dale said on TV, "It's a long way to trip Terreri."

On Glenn Hall:

My first year in Chicago I finally got a place in the dressing room. And my seat was right next to Glenn Hall. Before our first game, Glenn rushed into the bathroom and threw up. I didn't know he was renowned for this. So when he came back I said, "Glenn, do you get sick before every game?" And he growled back, "No, just since you joined the team."

Glenn delighted in getting on me when I was a rookie. In only my third game as a Blackhawk we were playing in New York and we had a big lead in the third period. I hadn't been on the ice at all when Billy Reay sent me out. The face-off was in the New York zone and Art Skov was the referee. Just before the puck was dropped Glenn Hall slapped his stick on the ice several times and Skov skated down to see what he wanted. Then he skated back to me and said, "Hall wants to see you."

Hell, I didn't know what to do so I skated down to see Glenn and by then the fans were going wild. You know how rotten the New York fans were. They were throwing things at me and yelling at the ref to drop the puck. When I skated up to Glenn he said, "Listen, rookie. Don't f— this game up." That was the message he delivered — short and sweet — and I sure tried hard not to f— things up.

On his dad, Robert Hull, Sr.:

My old man used to take the train from Belleville to Montreal whenever the Hawks played the Canadiens. And he'd hold court in the lobby of the old Mount Royal Hotel. He loved the attention he got for being Bobby Hull's father.

One time he went up to Bobby's room and he's putting on his coat to go to the Forum. Then he puts on a pair of toe rubbers and Lou Angotti, who was there, says, "Mr. Hull, I think those are my toe rubbers you're putting on." And the old man says, "Like hell, Angotti, I brought these toe rubbers from Belleville."

Well, you're not going to argue with him. Bobby had to go out and buy Louie another pair of toe rubbers.

I lost some shoes to him once. I went to visit him in Pointe Anne and I'd just bought a new pair of shoes. Threw my old ones away in the store. Now we go down to the waterfront and I take off my shoes to go barefoot. When it comes time for me to go, I look over and I see the old man has my shoes on. I say, "Hey, Dad, those are my shoes."

He says, "They are like hell. They're *my* shoes."

I said, "Well, where did my shoes go then?"

He says, "I don't know where the hell you put your shoes."

So I had to drive home barefoot that day. I only had those shoes for half an hour.

One time in Montreal he's sitting in the lobby of the Mount Royal. And to enter the hotel you have to walk up some steps. So my old man's there talking to the reporters and the fans, when he sees a man leading a German shepherd dog coming up the steps. He says in a loud voice, "Look at that son of a bitch. Bringing that dog into this nice hotel." And as the guy approaches you can see the dog is leading a blind man. My old man says in his booming voice, "Oh, the poor son of a bitch is blind." I say, "Yeah, Dad, but he's not deaf."

Now it's time to leave for the Forum and the old man jumps in a cab with Bobby and me. And the cabbie is happy to have Bobby Hull in his cab. And he's really polite with the old man. We reach the Forum and the cabbie says, "Better get out on the curb side, Mr. Hull. This is a one-way street and the traffic is fast. I don't want you getting hurt."

The old man growls, "Aw, the hell with that," and he yanks open the door and starts to get out when a passing car rips the door right out of his hand. He climbed out and walked away, cursing the cab and the cabbie and the "stupid Montreal drivers." Meanwhile, Bobby and I are scrambling to find enough money to pay the cabbie for the lost door.

The old man never figured any of his sons would make it in hockey. Or if he did he never told us. We'd come and visit him in the summer after we'd been in the NHL for a few years and Bobby had established himself as one of the greatest players in history. He'd just snort if someone mentioned our accomplishments and bellow out a line we'd heard so often, "I always said that neither one of you was any damn good."

The New Chicago Stadium

I T was in the fall of 1973 that Arthur and Bill Wirtz announced plans for an addition to Chicago Stadium, home of the Blackhawks, which would increase capacity from 20,000 to 30,000. Wow! That would give Chicago the largest indoor stadium in the world.

And those Wirtz fellows weren't kidding. There in a September 1973 issue of *The Hockey News* are photos of the model for the new-look Stadium. Mayor Richard J. Daley is in one photo, posing with Arthur Wirtz.

The addition was to be built over the east and west parking lots adjoining the Stadium with each providing 5,000 additional seats and 40,000 square feet of exhibition space.

"When the expansion of the building is complete in 1974 or 1975, it will be the only facility of its kind in the country that can cater to meetings of up to 30,000," said a spokesman for the project. "This means many added conventions and meetings will be coming to Chicago."

What happened to those grandiose plans? Well, they were discussed at meetings. Estimates were submitted. Months, then years slipped by and nothing more was done. By the nineties, the idea of adding to the old building was either forgotten, ignored, or written off as foolish. Nothing but a new arena would suffice. And soon Chicagoans had one — the spanking new United Center.

Nesterenko
Looks Back

I N the late '70s, Eric Nesterenko watched his first live hockey game in nearly five years. He described the 10–8 seesaw affair between Chicago and Toronto as "a travesty."

"I honestly couldn't remember when or if I'd ever seen a game in which 18 goals were scored," he said afterward. "Eighteen goals is boring. It means fans are watching terribly ragged play. Eighteen goals is basketball on ice. That night, fans were paying top dollars to see a pickup game on the pond and they couldn't have been enjoying it."

Nesterenko recalled his own playing days with the Hawks (1956–1972). The game, he maintains, was much different then.

"The NHL was comprised of the 100 finest players in the world and the fans knew who we were. They could identify us. They knew we belonged. The play was both elegant and brutal — but with intelligent violence, not the erratic, random mayhem of the fringe goons that new clubs hire to try to sell the game.

"What's more, the game was fashionable. Tickets were nearly impossible to get, a sure sign of status. People planned their social lives around games, even took winter vacations to follow games on the road. A game was an event. It was special theater. We could beat anyone and we often did. And if we lost it was never with apathy.

"Take that final playoff game in 1971. We lost to Montreal (rookie netminder Ken Dryden was awarded the Conn Smythe Trophy after the Habs won game seven by a 3–2 score) but not so much because they beat us but because we blew it. The stadium emptied. There wasn't a sound. The fans were suffering — injustice, rotten fates, passion thwarted. It was an incredible game, the crowd living and dying throughout and, when it was over, there was nothing to say. The catharsis was complete. I went to

O'Rourke's afterward to hide. It was that kind of bar, egalitarian, a hangout for non-sport freaks, and even there, there was talk. I sat quietly in a corner, exhausted, and became drunk very quickly."

In 1977, the game had changed so much and so quickly that Nesterenko realized he was no longer a part of it. And he vowed not to go too often to the past and fall into the trap that it used to be better.

"Too many teams, bad management, greed — these are powerful negatives against fine play," he stated. "As a rookie, one had to make the team every week for a year or two in order to belong, and one discovered quickly it was possible. I am no longer a part of it, and apparently many of the fans are no longer a part of it. Maybe it is part of a cycle happening throughout the sport. A growing up, a disillusionment that comes with middle age — and an acceptance of that state — that makes team games no longer the excruciating excitement they once were. Once, I belonged to the game. That was marvelous. Now it's over."

Orr's Last Skate

BY the fall of 1975, Bobby Orr's career with the Boston Bruins was thought to be over. Several operations — the first dating back to his rookie season in the NHL — had weakened his left knee to the point where he could no longer make his famous electrifying rushes up the ice. Orr endured two more painful operations that autumn, one in September 1975, another in November. Neither was successful. He was told that Lloyd's of London was unwilling to cover him for disability insurance because of the precarious state of his left knee. He played in only 10 games that season.

Despite the fact his chances of playing again with his old-time flair were slim, Orr's agent, Alan Eagleson, was demanding a huge pay hike from the Bruins. "A mere $200,000 per annum is not nearly enough for the game's greatest defenseman," Eagleson told Bruins general manager Harry Sinden.

Sinden hated to lose Orr but he said, "Sorry, it's not worth the risk."

There were other clubs hoping for a chance at Orr, should he become a free agent. They figured that Orr on one leg was better than anything they had on defense. One owner willing to pay big money for him was Bill Wirtz of the Chicago Blackhawks. Eagleson persuaded Wirtz, an old friend, to cough up a five-year contract worth $3 million.

Before he reported to the Hawks, Orr sparkled in the inaugural Canada Cup, played in September 1976 and won by Team Canada, He added a tournament MVP award to go with his eight Norris trophies, two Art Ross trophies, and numerous other honors. But the Canada Cup would be his last hurrah.

The long-term investment in Orr would not pay off for Wirtz and the Hawks. Playing conservatively and at about half his normal speed, Orr performed in only 20 games for Chicago during the 1976–77 season, scoring 4 goals and adding 19 assists.

In April 1977, his knee was opened up again and bony outcroppings were removed. The surgeons told him they'd done everything possible, and suggested that Orr stay off skates for a year.

He missed the entire 1977–78 season but tried to come back in the fall of 1978. After six games, frustrated and discouraged, he became the central figure at a press conference held at Chicago Stadium. Those of us who were there that day, holding microphones and facing cameras, were almost as choked with emotion as he was when he announced that his hockey career was over.

The man who had revolutionized the art of playing defense said he would skate no more. And when he spoke the words, there wasn't a dry eye in the room.

Stapleton's Got the Puck

EPTEMBER 28, 1972, has been called the most memorable date in hockey history. That was the day Team Canada conquered Russia in the now-famous eight-game series, with minister-to-be Paul Henderson slapping his own rebound past Soviet goaltending marvel Vladislav Tretiak — who would, years later, provide goaltending tutelage to young Blackhawk netminders.

Many assume that Henderson is the one who scooped up the precious memento of his game-winning goal, scored with 34 seconds to play in the final game.

"I wish I had," he says. "But it never occurred to me to pick it up. I was so ecstatic about scoring that goal and helping my team take the series that the puck seemed unimportant."

When the red light flashed behind Tretiak, the Canadian player closest to Henderson was Yvan Cournoyer. Perhaps he snared the puck. "No, no, I didn't get it," the Roadrunner says. "I didn't have a chance because Paul jumped into my arms."

Former Chicago Blackhawk Pat Stapleton claims with a sly grin that he owns the game-winning puck and has it "tucked away somewhere" in his farm home. Stapleton says that while all the Team Canada players were deliriously celebrating the victory, he calmly skated over and picked up the puck. And he has no plans to sell it, trade it, or let the kids in the neighborhood play a game of hockey with it.

Anyone doubting the veracity of Stapleton's claim should speak with Bill White. "I was there. I saw him pick it up," White says. "There's no doubt he has it. Collecting memorabilia runs in his family. His father collected a lot of baseball stuff over the years. It must be in Patty's genes."

Despite White's testimony, Stapleton's story must be taken with a grain of salt, since he was one of hockey's greatest pranksters and practical jokers. And White was often a willing accomplice.

During at least one Team Canada practice session in Moscow,

Stapleton recruited White to help him dazzle Soviet observers with a number of bizarre gyrations they called the "I Formation." The two Hawks would line up one behind the other on face-offs, and when the puck was dropped they'd twist, turn, and dart in different directions. None of it made any sense but Stapleton, with a perfectly straight face, called it the I Formation, or sometimes the Mohawk Formation, while the hometown observers scribbled notes furiously.

He also conned some of his teammates into getting on the tour bus for a special outing. "I've made arrangements for you guys to have golf privileges at the Moscow Golf and Country Club," he announced. "There'll be golf clubs for everybody and we'll start at the four-tiered driving range overlooking Gorky Boulevard." Two nights later he conned them again, convincing them he had reservations for his mates and their wives at Moscow's best Chinese restaurant. In 1972, how many foreigners knew that golf and Chinese food were nonexistent in the Soviet Union?

While Team Canada's players may remember Stapleton as the best practical joker they'd ever met, Chicago fans knew him for his solid defensive work on the Chicago blue line during the 1960s and '70s. Although small in stature, he, like fellow Hawk Pierre Pilote, was one of the best.

Fans may not recall that Stapleton was once team president, part owner, coach, and player in Chicago. But not with the Hawks: Patty held the various positions with the Chicago Cougars of the World Hockey Association.

"I loved playing for the Blackhawks and I loved the city of Chicago. But money talks and the WHA was offering more of it. Then there was the challenge of trying to make the new league a success. And frankly, I was concerned the Hawks were thinking of trading me. So I signed with the Cougars; I figured it would give me and my family a few more seasons in Chicago.

"Then, in my second season as a Cougar, the guys who owned the team simply walked away from hockey. So three of us — Ralph Backstrom, Dave Dryden, and myself — decided to buy the club. I wound up as part owner, club president, player, and coach. That lasted for less than one full season. After the team folded I played a couple of more years with Indianapolis and a final season with Cincinnati."

Any regrets about your career, Patty?

"No, I had a lot of thrills even though I never played on a Stanley Cup team. There was the Team Canada series in '72, winning in Moscow. And I was there again in '74 — when the WHA lost to the Soviets. With the Hawks, we came close to the Stanley Cup a couple of times. It just wasn't in the cards. But that's life, isn't it?"

7

The Hawks
Rebuild

Secord an Early Riser

WHEN he looks back on his days in minor hockey, Al Secord marvels that he ever did it. And that his parents were willing to do it.

He's talking about getting up at 4 a.m., pulling either his mom or his dad out of bed, standing around while they got the car warmed up, and having one or the other drive him to practice. He lived in Espanola, in Northern Ontario, and his Bantam team played its games in Sudbury — fifty miles away. And they practiced almost every morning from 6 o'clock until 7.

How many parents would consider the mere possibility of a career in pro hockey worth all that driving through some of the roughest winter weather imaginable? And how many kids would throw off the blankets at the first ring of the alarm, pull on some clothes, grab their hockey gear, and be ready to go? The Secords, parents and son, hardly gave it a second thought.

All that dedication, and all those practices, helped make Secord one of the best Junior players in the world. By 1975–76 he had graduated to the Hamilton Fincups of the Ontario Hockey Association, where he caught the eye of all the NHL scouts. In 1978, he was the top draft choice of the Boston Bruins, Number 16 overall.

He scored 16 goals in his rookie season, playing under coach Don Cherry, who tutored him well, and 23 goals as a sophomore under new coach Fred Creighton, who showed little confidence in him and gave him limited ice time.

Al says, "Sure I resented the treatment I received in Boston because I felt I never really had a fair chance to prove myself there."

In December 1980, when Harry Sinden had a chance to trade for Chicago defenseman Mike O'Connell and the Hawks asked for Secord in return, a deal was struck and Secord moved west. With the Hawks he scored 13 goals in 41 games and impressed people with his strong defensive play.

Then he really surprised everyone with some numbers that put him among the league's elite. He scored 44 goals one season and 54 the next. He scored four goals in one game and told reporters, "I'd like to see Harry Sinden's face when he hears about that." He later said he wished he hadn't popped off about Sinden because "it's not my style."

By then, Blackhawk fans began to wonder if he'd break some of Bobby Hull's scoring records. But in 1983–84 a strange abdominal injury, one slow to heal, kept him on the shelf for all but 14 games. The following season, still recuperating, he played in 51 games. He followed up with seasons of 40 and 29 goals before being traded to Toronto in 1987. He moved on to Philadelphia for a handful of games and wound up back in Chicago, signed as a free agent in 1989. He scored 14 goals in 43 games, then retired.

Pilous Misjudged the Great One

RUDY Pilous, a hockey man who prided himself on assessing teenage hockey players, the man who coached such Hall of Famers as Bobby Hull, Stan Mikita, Glenn Hall, and Pierre Pilote, misjudged the most prolific scorer of all time — Wayne Gretzky.

During the '70s, Pilous was general manager of the Winnipeg Jets of the World Hockey Association, with whom he won two Avco Cup championships. His biggest star was an aging Bobby

Hull, who had jumped from the Blackhawks to the Jets for an offer he couldn't refuse. But Pilous passed on a chance to land Gretzky, who would become an even bigger star.

In 1978, the teenage Gretzky had signed with Nelson Skalbania's WHA franchise in Indianapolis but when Skalbania, seeking ways to ease his financial problems, shopped the skinny centerman around the league, Pilous said he wasn't interested.

"The kid can't skate well enough to last long in pro hockey," he told Skalbania.

At least two NHL clubs, the Hawks and the Leafs, nodded in agreement. They had sent their scouts to watch Gretzky play in Birmingham one night. The scouts told their respective clubs that the skinny teenager was a mediocre skater who wouldn't stand up to NHL checking.

The kid who couldn't skate, and was too frail, went on to become the most prolific scorer in hockey history — beginning in Edmonton, a rival city.

Pilous was the last coach to lead Chicago to the Stanley Cup. He did it in 1961 when the Blackhawks downed the Red Wings four games to two in the finals.

It was a series in which two of the top scorers in history, Bobby Hull and Gordie Howe, were all but shut out. Hull scored twice in the opener and was blanked in the next five games. Howe scored only one goal in the finals.

A good Junior and Senior player, Pilous never made it to the NHL. In 1943, he founded and coached the St. Catharines Falcons, the Ontario city's first Junior A club. In 1954 he guided another Junior team from St. Catharines, the TeePees, all the way to the Memorial Cup.

"He excelled at the Junior level," said Pierre Pilote. "He sent a lot of players to the NHL and a lot of his boys became successful outside of hockey."

In Chicago, Pilous kept his instructions to a minimum. He'd say, "Let Bobby go with the puck" or "Let Stan play his game."

And he oozed color. In Montreal, he'd stir up the crowd with his hat-waving and his wisecracks. The Forum would erupt in catcalls and cries of "Pi-loo! Pi-loo!"

Pilous was angry and bitterly disappointed over his 1963

dismissal from the Blackhawks. He vowed never to set foot in Chicago Stadium again as long as he lived.

He was inducted into the Hockey Hall of Fame in 1985.

Bobby Comes Back

LONG after they retired from hockey, Bobby and Dennis Hull were in Chicago on business.

Bobby said to Dennis, "There's a game at the Stadium tonight. Do you want to go?"

Dennis said, "Sure I want to go."

Bobby said, "Do you think we can get tickets?"

"Bobby, I think they'll let us in without tickets. They might not let *me* in, but if I go with you I think they'll let us both in."

So they went to the game. And they got in.

Bobby said, "Where are we going to sit?"

"Why don't we sit in the press box?" Dennis suggested. "I think they'll let us in there, too."

They were welcomed into the press box and given choice seats.

In the old Chicago Stadium, the press box and its occupants were quite visible to the fans, and it wasn't long before a buzz went around the huge arena. "Bobby Hull's here tonight. He's sitting in the press box."

Dennis says, "The fans saw Bobby sitting there and suddenly more than 20,000 people began to rise. And they started to applaud and cheer, welcoming him back. Bobby hadn't been paying much attention and he said to me, 'What's going on? What did I miss?' And I nudged him. I said, 'They're cheering you, stupid. Stand up!'"

The ovation that followed was one of the longest in recent memory.

As a player, Bobby was acutely aware of his effect on the Chicago fans. He once said, "Any player who tells you they don't hear the fans must be deaf or asleep. I know that any time I picked up the puck behind the Chicago net, I heard 20,000 people start to hum and start to rise from their seats, and they went up the ice with me. I knew from the noise they made that they were out of their seats and were going up the ice behind me. So you see, I had absolutely no trouble getting the adrenaline flowing in Chicago. I knew that over 20,000 people were waiting for me to entertain them. Every professional player should think about that and come ready to play every game."

Where Are the Coaches?

IN the 1988 Stanley Cup playoffs, during game five of a series between the St. Louis Blues and the Chicago Blackhawks at the old St. Louis Arena, Chicago coach Bob Murdoch called for a strategy meeting during the second intermission. He and his assistants, Darryl Sutter and Wayne Thomas, entered a small room next to the Chicago dressing room. Murdoch, the last man in the room, slammed the door behind him. The coaches proceeded to talk about what they planned to do in the period ahead.

When the meeting broke up and Murdoch tried to open the door, it wouldn't budge — the lock had snapped into place and jammed. With the third period about to begin, the three coaches pounded on the door with their fists, hoping to attract attention to their plight. Arena workers, hearing the commotion, rushed to the scene and tugged on the doorknob. But the coaches remained entrapped.

By this time, players from both teams were skating slowly

around the ice, mystified by the delay, while the restless St. Louis fans clamored for a resumption of play.

Finally, an arena worker, driving a forklift up to the door, shouted a warning to the imprisoned occupants of the room to stand back. He barreled his vehicle into the heavy door, sending it flying. When the dust cleared, the three embarrassed coaches stepped over the rubble, dusted themselves off, and rushed to rinkside where they resumed their coaching duties.

Savard Should Have Been a Hab

IN June 1980 the Montreal Canadiens, who seldom erred at the draft table or anywhere else, astounded their fans. They had the first pick in the Entry Draft, and they elected not to claim hometown favorite Denis Savard, an immensely skilled francophone. Instead they chose Regina's Doug Wickenheiser.

Montrealers had already tabbed Savard, who scored 63 goals and 181 points in his final season of Junior hockey for the Montreal Junior Canadiens, as the logical heir to Hab legends like Rocket Richard and Guy Lafleur. They were stunned when the Montreal braintrust opted for a unilingual westerner.

The Blackhawks, drafting third, were overjoyed to bring Savard into the fold. Fortunately, he was still available because the Winnipeg Jets, with second choice, drafted another big man — defenseman David Babych.

Savard blossomed in a Chicago uniform, averaging 35 goals per season. He played in five All-Star games and topped 100 points five times. Over his entire 17-year NHL career he played in 1,196 games and scored 473 goals. Wickenheiser played for 10 seasons with five teams and scored 111 career goals.

Misjudging Savard's ability and potential was one of the greatest blunders in the history of the Montreal franchise. For the next decade they coveted the slick Hawk center, and when they finally pried him away from Chicago in 1990, when his career was in decline, the cost was enormous: they were forced to part with Chris Chelios, their best defenseman and a Norris Trophy winner. Chelios, a Chicago native, immediately cemented Chicago's defense while the Montreal power play ground to a halt without him.

TV analyst Don Cherry was astounded at the deal and was not shy about saying so.

"I'll tell you one thing," he said. "If Chelios's name had been Tremblay, the trade would never have happened. Lookit, Chelios is 28 and tough as nails. At his best in the clutch. Are you kiddin' me? Savard will soon be 30, right?"

Since the deal, Chelios has won two more Norris trophies. He's been named to five more All-Star teams. Now with Detroit, he's also been an All-Star in the Canada Cup and World Cup tournaments. Savard, meanwhile, drifted from Montreal to Tampa Bay and back to Chicago, where he finished his illustrious career in 1997.

When you think about Blackhawk draftees, Savard was perhaps their best ever. As a Junior he'd been voted MVP of the Quebec league in 1980. There he centered a line called "Les Trois Denis." He and both his wingers were named Denis — Denis Savard, Denis Cyr, and Denis Tremblay. What's more, all three were born on the same day — February 4, 1961. They grew up in the same neighborhood and played together all through minor hockey. Tremblay never turned pro, but Cyr played for six seasons in the NHL — with Chicago, Calgary, and St. Louis.

Praise for Pulford —
And a Kick in the Ass

READING Bob Pulford's biography in the Chicago Blackhawks media guide, you can't help but be impressed with the lengthy list of his hockey accomplishments:

- as a player, he was an outstanding penalty killer on four Stanley Cup teams in Toronto;
- Pulford was named NHL coach of the year after leading Los Angeles to 105 points in the 1974–75 season;
- taking the reins as head coach and general manager of the Blackhawks, in July 1977, he was named coach of the year by *The Hockey News* in his first season;
- his teams won eight division titles and made the playoffs in each of his first twenty years with Chicago;
- on June 21, 1991, he was elected to the Hockey Hall of Fame;
- he now serves as senior vice president of the Hawks and — at the time of this writing — as general manager and head coach.

Despite these credentials, a heavy dose of criticism was leveled at him in *The Hockey News* in July 1988. It came from one of Pulford's harshest critics, Eric Duhatschek.

He began by castigating Pulford for firing Bob Murdoch, "a decent, hard-working man . . . after uprooting him from Calgary with words like commitment and promise and future."

Duhatschek continues:

> You're Bob Pulford and you realize what a mess you've made of your minor-league system. Steve Larmer arrived in

1982 and nobody of any consequence has been developed in the system since then.

You're Bob Pulford and you flinch when you read Page 6 of your yearbook, about how "you are respected as one of the brightest general managers in the NHL," about how you "take a back seat to no one when it comes to putting a winning team on the ice."

Idly, you skim over the eleven years of your administration and try to remember what that phrase — winning hockey — means.

You glance at your trade record and wince: did I really trade Carey Wilson for Denis Cyr? Tony Tanti for Curt Fraser? Doug Crossman and a second-round draft choice (Scott Mellanby) for Behn Wilson?

Did I really turn down Brett Hull, the budding young star, when Calgary was shopping him around the league? Hull, the kid with the dynamite name and the heavy slap shot, who could fill my building for years to come?

You page ahead to your draft record and now you really shudder. Did I really take Keith Brown ahead of Ray Bourque in 1979? Jerome Dupont ahead of Brent Sutter in 1980? Ken Yaremchuk ahead of Dave Andreychuk in 1982? Dave Manson when I could have had Sean Burke or Joe Nieuwendyk in 1985?

You say a second prayer of thanks because in the last eleven years your team played four seasons in the Smythe Division, when it was the league's patsy, and seven in the sad-sack Norris Division.

You kick yourself because you couldn't see — the way good managers did — the direction in which the game was headed.

You didn't anticipate — as Montreal Canadiens did — the value of drafting players out of, or heading to, U.S. colleges. So in 1981, you got Kevin Griffin, they got Chris Chelios.

You didn't envision — as Calgary Flames did — that it was possible to build the supporting cast of a winning team around college free agents. Joel Otto, Jamie Macoun, Colin

Patterson, Neil Sheehy, Gino Cavallini — all came cheaply to Calgary.

You weren't in on the first, or even second, wave of the European migration. You try to recall if you dozed off when foreign names began to crop up on the draft lists of the teams that did win championships. Names like Kurri and Tikkanen in Edmonton, Naslund in Montreal. Persson and Jonsson on the Islanders.

You look up at the autographed picture of Don Cherry on your office wall and know of one man anyway who applauds your perfect record of xenophobia. Not one European-trained player (at this writing) has ever worn Chicago's red, black, and white.

You consider your new coach, Mike Keenan, and wonder how Denis Savard will respond to his heavy-handed tactics. You think about the orders to fire Murdoch that came from the executive offices and consider that your authority may finally be slipping away.

You're Bob Pulford and you wonder why you are still working in this business.

I wonder, too.

Former Hawk Dennis Hull tosses another dart at Pulford's hide:

I asked Pulford one day years ago if he was going to draft my nephew Brett Hull.

"No, the kid's too slow."

Another time I asked him if he was interested in Doug Gilmour, who'd just led the Ontario Hockey League in scoring for Cornwall.

"No, the kid's too small."

Hey, Dennis, don't forget a kid named Gretzky. It was a Chicago scout who saw Gretzky perform in the WHA one night and convinced Pulford he was both of the above — too slow and too small — and too fragile — ever to make it in the NHL.

Roenick a Phenom

WHEN he was a 16-year-old sophomore at Thayer Academy in Braintree, Massachusetts, Jeremy Roenick was rated the top player in his age group by the U.S. Amateur Hockey Association.

NHL scouts were amazed at the skills of the young phenom, whose parents had moved from Virginia to New England to give their son a better chance to hone his skills and to cut down on travel costs that were destroying the family budget. (As a 14-year-old Roenick had been boarding a plane every weekend to join the New Jersey Rockets for games played all over North America.)

At Thayer in 1986, Roenick wasn't the only hockey star on his team. One of his teammates was Tony Amonte, a kid who was almost as highly rated.

"Some people say I play like Wayne Gretzky," Roenick said at the time. "Then others compare me to Mario Lemieux. I just say no matter how good you are there's always someone better."

A scout for the Quebec Nordiques likened Roenick to Guy Lafleur and predicted a "phenomenal career" for him: "I'm convinced he'll be the Number 1 player drafted in the 1988 Entry Draft," he stated.

As it turned out, he wasn't chosen first overall. That honor went to Mike Modano, who was taken by Minnesota. But Roenick wasn't far down the ladder. Quebec messed up by taking Daniel Dore (2 goals in a 17-game career) fifth overall, and Toronto overrated Scott Pearson, claiming him with the sixth pick, allowing Chicago to claim Roenick eighth overall.

Roenick was an instant hit and a huge fan favorite for the Hawks. He was brought up for 20 games in 1988–89 and collected 18 points. The following year, he jumped to 26 goals and 66 points. In 1990–91 he scored 41 goals and in 1991–92 he hit for 53 goals and led the Hawks in points with 103. Back-to-back 107-point seasons followed.

By 1995–96 he had become the eighth-leading scorer in Chicago history, but a contract hassle weighed on his mind, affected his play, and his production fell off. As a Group 2 free agent he began to think about faraway fields and how much greener they looked. His agent, Neil Abbott, scoffed at a five-year, $17.5 million offer from the Hawks. Abbott pointed to Roenick's former teammate Joe Murphy, a 22-goal scorer, who had jumped to St. Louis for three years and $10 million. "Do I even have to ask what that does for Jeremy's price?" he sneered.

Meanwhile Roenick, who'd slumped to 32 goals, said he was unappreciated by the Chicago brass and made it clear he was unwilling to return — no matter what Pulford might throw on the table.

Pulford had no choice but to trade one of the most popular players in his team's history. After lengthy negotiations with the New York Islanders, he turned to the Phoenix Coyotes and suddenly a trade took shape. On August 16, 1996, Roenick became a Coyote in return for unhappy centerman Alexei Zhamnov, plus a first-round 1997 draft pick (Ty Jones) and Craig Mills, a 20-year-old right wing prospect.

Ironically, Zhamnov had been demanding a trade, threatening to play in Europe. Why? Because Phoenix wouldn't compensate him in the amount of $2.6 million, the salary teammate Keith Tkachuk was earning.

Which team got the better of the deal?

Entering the 2000–2001 season, Roenick, now 30, has scored 111 goals and 275 points as a Coyote, while Zhamnov, 30, has scored 84 goals and 232 points as a Hawk.

Remember
Mount Orval?

DO you recall Orval Tessier and his brief stint as coach of the Hawks? The 49-year-old did a remarkable job in 1982–83, his first season behind the Blackhawk bench. He elevated them from 30 wins and 72 points to 47 wins and 104 points. It was their best showing in nine years and Tessier earned much of the credit for the Hawks' first-place finish in the Norris Division. He was named coach of the year by both the NHL and *The Hockey News*.

"Orval has been a winner everywhere he's coached," Bob Pulford said when he promoted Tessier from the AHL to the NHL. "He was a successful coach in Junior hockey and as a first-year pro coach he guided New Brunswick to the AHL championship and a Calder Cup victory."

In the 1983 playoffs, with Tessier wheeling Chicago toward a Stanley Cup, the Hawks ousted the Blues and the North Stars, losing only two of nine games. Then they met Wayne Gretzky and the Edmonton Oilers in the Campbell Conference finals and the wheels came spinning off Tessier's chariot.

Edmonton blew past Chicago in four straight games, leaving the Hawks stunned and speechless. All but Tessier, who had a lot to say.

After the first two humiliating defeats at the hands of Gretzky and his chums, by scores of 8–4 and 8–2, Tessier earned a new nickname: Mount Orval. Like a volcano he blew sky-high and told the press his players "needed eighteen heart transplants." Although some tried to shrug them off, his words stung the Hawks. Al Secord engaged in a stormy dressing-room confrontation with the coach before the Hawks were eliminated, suffering two more losses at the Stadium.

Members of the media gleefully called the irate coach "Lava Lips" and "The Glowering Inferno."

Orval shrugged and said, "Too many people took my tirades the wrong way. You gotta live with what you say. No question about it. If I could have taken the remark back I would have. It wasn't meant the way it came out but when it was done it was done. And that doesn't bother me whatsoever."

But after his controversial comments he never again got the best out of his Hawks. Within a year and a half, after the Hawks slipped from 104 points to 68, Tessier got the pink slip from Bob Pulford.

Don Cherry, who was also the talkative sort when he coached the Boston Bruins, said, "If ever there was a guy who deserved to lose his job it was Tessier. That heart transplant comment he made, the players playing their hearts out for him and all that. Then he turns on them when they lose. He had some strange ideas. Can you believe former Hawks (weren't even allowed) in the dressing room? You ask me, Tessier got what he deserved."

After his stormy two-and-a-half-season reign as Chicago coach, Tessier returned to his roots in Cornwall, Ontario, where he again became involved in Junior hockey.

"Orval's the best thing that happened to our team this year," wrote Claude McIntosh, sports editor of the local paper. "I think he's learned from his experience in Chicago. Learned you've got to be very discreet with the media."

If Tessier was any mellower back in Junior it wasn't apparent to some of his players. Two who broke curfew one night heard a lecture the next day that blistered their ears in the Cornwall dressing room.

Writing in The Hockey News, Bob McKenzie said of Tessier:

When he got fired, it seems that no one had a nice word to say about him. And it's certainly true that some players never forgave him for his "heart transplant" zinger.

But the man should get credit where credit is due. So every time crafty winger Steve Larmer scores a goal, chalk one up for Orval. It was said that Larmer wasn't strong enough or fast enough to play in the NHL. Those were the raps against him when he was selected 120th overall in his draft year, despite outstanding numbers in Junior hockey. But the Peterborough native went on to have a great rookie season in the AHL with the Tessier-coached New Brunswick Hawks. And when Orval got the call to move up to Chicago, he took Larmer with him.

A Decade
of Instability

Goulet's Career Ends in Near Disaster

ICHEL Goulet's magnificent NHL career came to a sad and sudden end in Montreal on March 16, 1994.

When he slammed headfirst into the Forum boards, with only a flimsy helmet protecting his head, he suffered a concussion that left those who witnessed it in shock. He struck the boards with such force that the accident might well have ended his life.

After spending more than a week in hospital, Goulet continued to be plagued by severe headaches, dizziness, and memory loss. He felt like he'd been jumped on by a herd of elephants.

Gradually he recovered, and he began working out again in the off-season, hoping he'd be able to re-establish himself as one of the most potent left wingers in hockey.

"I trained all summer and did all the therapy the doctors prescribed, but when I got to training camp I knew something was missing. I wasn't quite myself. The other guys were just too fast. I knew then, after sixteen years in professional hockey, it was time for me to step aside.

"The team doctors told me I'd failed the physical. They said it was too dangerous for me to continue because another blow to the head like the one I suffered in Montreal could be fatal."

Although he came to the Hawks late in his career, Goulet will be remembered as one of the greatest scorers in NHL history. He scored 548 career goals and 604 assists. As a star with the Quebec Nordiques in the 1980s, he had four 50-goal seasons.

Jeremy Roenick was sad to see his linemate say goodbye to hockey.

"He meant so much to my career," Roenick told writer Tim Sassone. "He taught me the smarts of the game, where to be, how to handle the media, what it's like to be a big-name player. He is a very special person."

Goulet said the greatest moment in his hockey career was reaching the Stanley Cup finals with the Blackhawks in 1992, even though he walked away without a ring or his name on the Cup.

When he was inducted into the Hockey Hall of Fame in 1998, Goulet recalled being with a group of 500-goal scorers in Atlantic City a few years ago. "I was there with Jean Beliveau, Bobby Hull, and Gordie Howe. I was the youngest player there. I was just a kid when Beliveau scored his 500th and I remember thinking, someday I will score 500 NHL goals. I was 10 years old at the time."

An Ugly Blow

I T happened in a game played just after Christmas — on December 29, 1992 — at Joe Louis Arena in Detroit.

Chicago's Jocelyn Lemieux was checking Red Wing defenseman Vladimir Konstantinov in the neutral zone when the Hawk player suffered an agonizing and preventable injury.

Konstantinov brought his stick up and smashed Lemieux squarely in the mouth, knocking out a couple of teeth. The resulting damage to Lemieux's mouth and gums took a surgeon's skill to repair. It took 110 stitches, most of them in the lips and mouth, to sew up the jagged gash that marred his features.

"I could feel a big hole in my lip and I remember the wood of the stick crashing into my teeth," Lemieux said. "And of course there was an immense amount of pain. When I felt a big chunk of skin against my teeth I knew I'd suffered an ugly, scary injury.

"Maybe I should have kept my stick up to protect myself. Maybe I was stupid not to. I may be a bit of an instigator but I'd never do that to another player. Never. And the guy didn't even get a penalty. Often they call five-minute majors when you just tap a guy with your stick. And the referee, Ron Hoggarth, misses something like this. It's unbelievable.

"But Konstantinov will learn. Maybe when someone takes his knee out. He's like Ulf Samuelsson. He's known as a dirty player."

Konstantinov, who was known as Bad Vlad or Vlad the Impaler because of his reputation as a ferocious checker, was runner-up for the Norris Trophy four-and-a-half years later, in 1997. But after the Red Wings' Stanley Cup triumph that spring he was brain-damaged in a horrific limousine accident after a team golf outing and party. He'll never play hockey, never lead a normal life again.

Chelios Pops Off, Takes Off

CHRIS Chelios, a Chicago native with a lifelong passion for hockey, was disturbed and angry when the 1994–95 NHL season failed to start on time. A bitter dispute between the league owners, represented by commissioner Gary Bettman, and the NHL Players Association, headed by Bob Goodenow, ultimately kept players off the ice for 103 days. Just as negotiators on both sides were about to declare the season lost, an agreement was reached on various issues and an abbreviated 48-game schedule began on January 20, 1995.

Never one to hide his emotions, Chelios delivered a verbal assault on commissioner Bettman early in the dispute that shocked the hockey community.

In a televised interview he said, "If I was Gary Bettman, I'd be worried about my family. I'd be worried about my well-being.

Some crazed fans — or even a player, who knows? — might take matters into their own hands and get him — and league vice president Brian Burke — out of the way."

"I took it pretty personal that we weren't going to be playing hockey for some time," he later tried to explain.

The quote stunned Chelios's agent, Tom Reich. "I characterized it as tackling a guy 10 yards out of bounds with a forearm to the head," Reich said in dismay. "It was way beyond the bounds of behavior and Chris quickly understood that."

On the day after the interview, Chelios phoned Bettman to apologize for his ill-chosen remarks. He also apologized to Chicago owner Bill Wirtz.

"It was never meant to be a threat," he said. "There is no way I would wish anything bad on anybody. It was just a comment — a very bad comment." He added, "I try hard to be a good role model for kids because I love kids. I made a big mistake and I know I'll make up for it. I'll do anything for hockey."

After the comments garnered international attention, Chelios started to give deep thought to his actions. "I never wanted to have an image like that," he said. "Never wanted to have mine tarnished like that."

His penalty minutes dropped dramatically. He vowed he'd never again take 51 minutes in one game, as he had one night in 1993–94 when he was tagged with three minors, one major, two 10-minute misconducts, two game misconducts, and a match penalty.

NHL forward Brian Propp once said of Chelios, "He's the kind of guy who will stick your eye out and not care." Propp may have been referring to an incident in 1993–94 when Chelios raked the eyes of Vancouver defenseman Dana Murzyn. He also attacked a linesman, Bernard DeGrace, and received suspensions for both assaults, costing himself close to $100,000 in salary.

In 1998–99, at age 37 and having collected three Norris trophies, Chelios made it known he wanted to finish his career in Chicago. And general manager Bob Murray said he had no intention of trading his star defenseman. Chelios even had a handshake agreement with Chicago owner Bill Wirtz that he couldn't be dealt.

But three days before the trade deadline, Chelios apparently had a change of heart. His agent, Steve Reich, asked Murray for permission to speak with teams that might extend his client's contract in the event of a trade.

Murray, claiming to be stunned by the request and the sudden turn of events, quickly arranged a trade with Detroit. He sent Chelios to the Red Wings in return for defenseman Anders Eriksson and two first-round draft choices. "The bottom line was, it turned out to be all about money," Murray said.

"Not true," replied Chelios from Detroit. "It wasn't about money. It was about feeling wanted."

Still, the money couldn't be ignored. Chelios received a whopping two-year, $11 million contract extension from the Red Wings.

"Chris has all the security in the world now," said Murray. "He should be happy. He just made himself $11 million. And I think he should thank Mr. Wirtz."

A Stunning Playoff Defeat

IN the spring of 1991, the Blackhawks and their fans were contemplating the possibility of a Stanley Cup parade, the fourth in team history and the first since Bobby Hull, Stan Mikita, and Company brought home hockey's most coveted trophy three decades earlier, in 1961.

Their Cup hopes were quite realistic. Coach Mike Keenan demanded, and got, maximum effort from his talented crew that season. Ed Belfour topped all goaltenders with a 2.47 goals-against average and a club record of 43 wins. At the other end of the rink, the Hawks boasted potent offense from Steve Larmer

(44 goals), Jeremy Roenick (41), Michel Goulet (27), and Dirk Graham (24). All were largely responsible for a first-place finish in the overall standings (106 points). Why wouldn't the Hawks be favored to wrestle Lord Stanley's old basin away from all other contenders?

Chicago expected little opposition in the opening playoff round. Their opponents, the Minnesota North Stars, had finished with a mere 68 points and had won 22 fewer games than the Hawks.

The North Stars squeezed out a 4–3 overtime victory in game one, but the Hawks recovered to tie the series with a 5–2 win. They followed with a 6–5 victory, but stumbled in game four, a 3–1 defeat. The fifth game of the series was an unexpected disaster. The Stars blanked the Hawks 6–0 and, buoyed by that convincing shutout, came right back with a 3–1 win in game six. Suddenly the mighty Hawks, a team ticketed for hockey glory, found themselves bound for the golf course. It marked the first time in twenty years that a team finishing first overall had been bounced from the postseason in the opening round.

The Hawks agreed they should be ashamed of themselves for their undisciplined play. It was easy to pinpoint the reason for their quick demise. Throughout the series, Keenan's belligerent troops beat a steady path to the penalty box, with 91 (count 'em) banishments in the six games. The North Stars took full advantage of all this foolishness, scoring 15 goals on 54 power plays (a record number in a playoff series).

"This is tougher to take than anything I've been associated with," said center Troy Murray. "In all the years I've been here, I've never seen the team play so confused. We were always doing the wrong thing at the wrong time."

How stunning was Chicago's loss to a club that finished 16th overall? It was the most shocking playoff upset since the Los Angeles Kings knocked Edmonton out in 1982, after the Oilers finished 48 points ahead of the Kings.

Pierre Pilote won the Norris Trophy as the NHL's best defenseman three consecutive years, from 1963 to 1965.

The author with Stan Mikita prior to a game at Maple Leaf Gardens. Mikita is still the only player to have won three major trophies in one season — the Ross, the Hart, and the Lady Byng — and he did it twice!

— Dave Cooper

In 1967, Hawk Phil Esposito was the central figure in what became known as hockey's most lopsided trade. Soon after, he became a huge star with the Boston Bruins.

Bill Mosienko celebrates the third goal in his famous hat trick — three goals in 21 seconds. The hapless goalie is rookie Ranger Lorne Anderson.

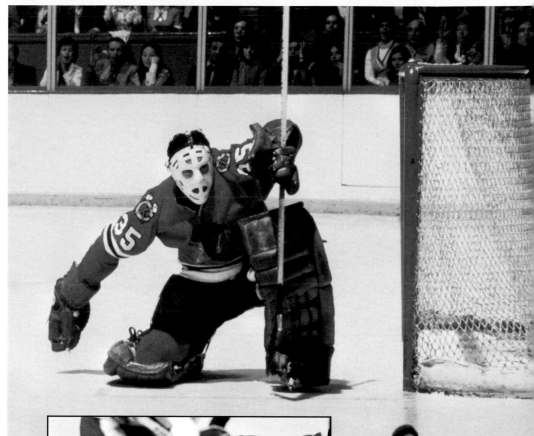

Goalie Tony Esposito deflects a shot. In 1969–70, Esposito set a modern-day record with 15 shutouts in one season. He won both the Calder and the Vezina for his efforts.

In the 1980 entry draft, Montreal erred by failing to select hometown hero Denis Savard. Chicago, drafting third, grabbed him. Savard went on to become one of hockey's greatest scorers.

— Robert B. Shaver

*Defenseman Doug Wilson played in seven All-Star games (six as a Hawk)
from 1982 to 1992, and captured the Norris Trophy in 1982.*

*Hall of Famer Bob Pulford
has been a coach or
manager with the Hawks
for almost 25 years.*

*Calder Trophy–winner
Steve Larmer holds one of
the longest consecutive
game streaks in NHL
history, at 884 games, 80
games shy of the NHL
record held by Doug Jarvis.*

— Ray Grabowski

Chicago-born defenseman Chris Chelios, acquired from Montreal for Denis Savard in 1990, captured the Norris Trophy three times, twice as a Hawk.
— Ray Grabowski

Jeremy Roenick and Brian Noonan, both Boston-born, celebrate a goal against the San Jose Sharks. That's former Hawk Doug Wilson on the left.
— Ray Grabowski

*As a Chicago rookie in 1990–91, Eddie "The Eagle" Belfour won
43 games, breaking Tony Esposito's club record. Belfour, like
Esposito 21 years before, won both the Calder and the Vezina.*

— Ray Grabowski

Right winger Tony Amonte has become the Blackhawks' leader and a fan favorite. He led the Hawks in 1999–2000 with 43 goals.

Keenan Ruffles Feathers

N July 1991, forward Troy Murray quietly left the Blackhawks, having been traded to the Winnipeg Jets. Murray, who had tallied a career-high 45 goals and 99 points for the Hawks in 1985–86, went out of his way to thank Bob Pulford and Bill Wirtz for treating him well in Chicago. But he had little to say about Mike Keenan, then the Hawks' coach and general manager.

Two months later, forward Wayne Presley was gone, too — traded to San Jose for a third-round draft choice. Presley, who had scored 32 goals and 61 points in 1986–87 and had never come close to those totals again, blasted Keenan as he left.

"Mike and I have a personality conflict," he complained. "I never got much support from him. I want to score 30 goals again."

He never would, averaging a little more than 10 goals per season over the next five years. Murray's goal production was even worse in the five additional seasons he played.

Perhaps Keenan, peering into a crystal ball, was able to see the erosion of the traded players' skills long before anyone else.

It was Doug Wilson's turn next. The 14-year veteran and 1982 Norris Trophy winner was the Hawks' all-time leading defenseman in goals (225), assists (554), and points (779). He was dealt to San Jose. "I'm elated to be leaving," he said. "To go to the rink every day and not enjoy it was something I couldn't imagine. No team worked harder than we did and no team had less fun." While he didn't mention Keenan by name, the inference was clear.

"I'm more saddened by the treatment Denis Savard received before he was traded to Montreal," Wilson added, referring to a well-publicized feud between Savard and Keenan that only ended when the star center was shipped to the Habs for Chris Chelios. "No one should have had to go through what Denis did."

Keenan was quick to fire back. "I'm tired of all this bullshit," he spat. "All I know is we went from last place to first. The bottom line is we didn't win with Savard and Wilson. Doug was in

Chicago for fourteen years and didn't win anything. As for having fun, I coached Gretzky, Messier, Paul Coffey, and others in the Canada Cup. They think winning is fun. As for the Savard deal, ask the guys who they'd rather play with, Denis Savard or Chris Chelios?"

Keenan's next deal sent defenseman Dave Manson to Edmonton for rearguard Steve Smith. Manson, who'd had disagreements with his coach — including a shoving match — fired a parting shot at Keenan. "Some days some of us feared coming to the rink (in Chicago)."

Keenan might well have countered that there were days when Manson wasn't even allowed *on* the rink. In 1988–89 he was suspended four different times for on-ice indiscretions and missed 19 games.

Soon after the 1991–92 season began, Trent Yawney, another defenseman, walked out on the club and demanded a trade. He complained that Keenan was not giving him enough playing time and vowed never to play for the Hawks again. After a six-week absence he agreed to play for the Hawks' farm team in Indianapolis. Keenan traded him to Calgary in December 1991 for Stephane Matteau.

Another unhappy Hawk was goalie Dominik Hasek, a three-time player of the year in his native Czechoslovakia. He was sent to Indianapolis when Keenan opted to stick with Ed Belfour. Hasek's agent, Rich Winter, said, "Dominik was an all-star in the minors last season, not Waite. If he was given a ten-game chance he'd make it to the All-Star Game." When Hasek, then 26, finally got a chance in 1991–92 he went 10–4–1 and made the NHL All-Rookie team. But he vowed he wouldn't be in Chicago long if Keenan didn't give him more game action. Since the Hawks seemed set in goal with Ed Belfour, Keenan shipped Hasek to Buffalo for Stephane Beauregard and a draft choice, with which the Hawks drafted Eric Daze.

In April 1992, Bryan Marchment erupted after Keenan scratched him from a game. To show his displeasure, Marchment threw a thirty-pound dumbbell through a mirror in the Chicago dressing room.

Despite the turmoil within the ranks, Keenan led the Hawks

to a record-tying 11 consecutive playoff wins before his team was swept by Pittsburgh in the 1992 Stanley Cup finals.

Probert Deal a Costly Mistake

WHEN he was a member of the Detroit Red Wings, no player messed up more thoroughly than Bob Probert. During his stint with the Wings (1985–86 to 1993–94):

- customs agents found 14.1 grams of cocaine in his underwear;
- he was charged with smuggling narcotics into the United States;
- he was banned from entering the United States and expelled from the NHL;
- he twice left a substance-abuse center without authorization — once with the help of another player's wife;
- his driver's license was revoked;
- he was sentenced to three months in prison, three months probation, and fined $2,000 for cocaine smuggling;
- a Chicago immigration judge ordered him deported to Canada;
- another judge ordered him not to cross the border into Canada;
- he played for a prison hockey club;
- he visited schools urging students to stay clear of drugs;
- he was reinstated by NHL president John Ziegler;
- he missed one full season and earned a prolonged ovation when he returned;
- he served more than 2,000 minutes in penalties.

In July 1994, Probert left the Red Wings as a free agent and signed a contract with the Chicago Blackhawks. In his first year as a Hawk he did not play, but spent months in a rehab center in California while the club picked up the $5,000-per-week tab.

During the next four seasons, his skills beginning to deteriorate markedly, he went from 19 goals, to 9, to 2, to 7.

Incredibly, the Hawks handed the 33-year-old Probert a three-year extension on his contract at the end of the 1997–98 season. It was a huge mistake.

Prior to the 1999–2000 season, general manager Bob Murray asked Probert to take a cut in salary from $1.7 million to $1 million.

Probert just laughed. "No way," he said. "If I have to go to the minors, I'll go there."

Reluctantly, Murray kept him around. Then, early in the season, Probert lost more than $33,000 of his salary when he was suspended for striking goalie Steve Shields of the San Jose Sharks.

In 1999–2000, Probert scored only 4 goals in 11 games and reached a milestone when he surpassed 3,000 minutes in penalties — only the sixth player in NHL history to top that plateau.

But more importantly, he reached another significant milestone off the ice by completing his sixth year of being clean and sober, making his on-ice efforts pale in comparison.

"What Bob has done with his life is outstanding," said Bob Pulford. "I think people who can turn their lives around deserve our pride and respect."

Don't Mess with Wirtz

IN 1995 the Chicago Blackhawks thought they'd made a great deal. They quietly traded disgruntled forward Jeremy Roenick to the Winnipeg Jets for holdout winger Keith Tkachuk.

Both players had been Number 1 draft choices by their respective clubs and both were capable of 50-goal seasons.

But the deal never was consummated. Apparently, Jets owner Barry Shenkarow changed his mind at the last minute about trading Tkachuk when he heard through the grapevine that Roenick was lukewarm to a move north to Manitoba. Bill Wirtz and Bob Pulford promptly accused Shenkarow of reneging on the deal.

By September 1995, when Tkachuk had become a Group 2 free agent, Wirtz moved in and signed the star to a five-year, $17.2 million (U.S.) offer sheet. Tkachuk stood to earn a hefty $6 million in the first year of the deal.

The offer was a blunt message from Wirtz to Shenkarow: "Don't mess with me."

League rules provided the Jets with three options. They could match the astonishing offer and retain Tkachuk's services; they could try to work out a trade with the Hawks; or they could accept five first-round draft choices as compensation for Tkachuk.

Before Tkachuk could run to the bank, try on a Blackhawks jersey, or even find his way to the Chicago dressing room, the Jets hollered, "Wait a minute. This isn't a done deal. We can keep this guy."

They could — and they did — but at a staggering price.

The cash-poor Jets decided to match the offer, making Tkachuk the highest-paid player in Canada at almost $8 million in Canadian funds.

Shenkarow retained his star player, but he soon lost his team. Within days he announced the club would be sold for $65 million (U.S.) and would be moved from Winnipeg to Phoenix at the end of the 1995–96 season.

After raising the ire of Bill Wirtz, he was probably happy to get out of hockey. And Wirtz was glad to see him go.

Amonte Still Mourns Missed Cup Win

―――――――――――

WHEN the New York Rangers won the Stanley Cup in 1994, it ended 54 years of misery for the Blueshirts' fans. It also marked the beginning of a long lament for Tony Amonte.

Amonte was traded to the Chicago Blackhawks three months before the Rangers' victory. Mike Keenan, then the coach of the Rangers, unloaded the third-year NHLer for proven veterans Brian Noonan and Stephane Matteau. The trade couldn't have come at a better time for those two, or at a worse time for Amonte.

Even though it's been six years since the deal, Amonte still cringes at the mention of the Rangers' championship. In an interview with Mike Brophy of *The Hockey News*, he admitted: "I still think about it . . . all the time. Especially the last two years when (the Blackhawks have) been out of the playoffs. I mean, I was *that* close in New York. Now I'm beginning to feel that time is running out for me. I'm turning 30, and for hockey players, that means the end is in sight."

Amonte has seldom had reason to be discouraged about his hockey career. When New York drafted him 68th overall in 1988, Scotty Bowman compared him to former Montreal Canadien Yvan Cournoyer — because of his speed and the fact that he's a left-hand shot who plays the right wing.

In his first eight NHL seasons, Amonte has earned millions, played in four All-Star games, scored 30 or more goals six times, and scored the tournament-winning goal for the U.S. in the 1996 World Cup of Hockey. The 1999–2000 season was his best to date: Amonte scored 43 goals and 41 assists in 82 games. He's closing in on 300 career goals and his speed alone should make him a fixture in the NHL for years to come.

So why is Amonte so frustrated with Chicago? The Blackhawks

haven't won the Stanley Cup since 1961 and their next one may not come until Amonte is old and feeble. For now, he's stuck in Chicago — his contract doesn't expire until 2002, at which time he'll be an unrestricted free agent. Still, he is a team player who gives it his all in every game. When he was asked about his commitment to the Blackhawks, he said, "I love Chicago and I try to remain optimistic. I have faith we can turn things around."

Larmer's Streak Ends on Bitter Note

WHEN the Chicago Blackhawks prepared to open the 1993–94 NHL season, star right winger Steve Larmer was working out in a Chicago industrial league.

Making it clear that he was unhappy with his role in Chicago and with the direction head coach Darryl Sutter was taking the Hawks, Larmer requested a trade during the 1993 off-season. Since Sutter was a friend, Larmer had decided it would be better to play on another team's ice.

But general manager Bob Pulford wanted Larmer to stay, and offered him a handsome salary to remain in the Hawk fold. Entering the option year of a four-year contract, Larmer turned Pulford down, figuring he was worth $4 million for three seasons with a new team.

The Chicago braintrust had five months to work out a trade, but failed to move the veteran, leaving him bitter and upset.

When the Hawks opened the season on October 6, 1993, against Florida, Larmer was missing from the lineup. His absence that night brought to an end one of the longest consecutive-game streaks in NHL history — 884 games, only 80 shy of Doug Jarvis's league record.

Thirteen games into the season, Pulford sent Larmer and defenseman Bryan Marchment to the Hartford Whalers for winger Patrick Poulin and defenseman Eric Weinrich. The Whalers immediately flipped Larmer, Nick Kypreos, and Barry Richter, along with a second-round draft choice, to the New York Rangers for defenseman James Patrick and forward Darren Turcotte.

It was Ranger coach Mike Keenan who coveted Larmer. Having coached him in Chicago from 1988 to 1992, Keenan said that "Larmer is a leader on the ice and a very fine individual. I'm delighted to have him on my team."

Larmer put the loss of the iron-man streak behind him, responded with 21 goals in what was left of the season and added 9 more in the playoffs, helping the Rangers win the Stanley Cup. He came back the next year to score 14 goals in 47 games during a lockout-shortened season, then called it quits.

Over his 1,006-game NHL career, Larmer averaged just over a point a game. Even though he wonders what might have been, whether he'd have broken Jarvis's record if he'd remained a Blackhawk, the thrill of a Stanley Cup victory more than made up for any loss he may have felt.

Wirtz Livid, Team Doctor Quits

D URING the first round of the 1997 playoffs, the Chicago Blackhawks were hit with a rash of injuries in their series with the Colorado Avalanche. As part of the fallout, team doctor Louis Kolb walked off the job in the middle of game three after being castigated by team owner Bill Wirtz — who, among other things, accused Kolb of conspiring to aid the Avalanche cause.

First, Wirtz accused Kolb of mistreating center Alexei Zhamnov's ankle injury. Then he censured Kolb for misdiagnosing an injury to Brent Sutter, claiming the doctor allowed Sutter to play with a torn anterior cruciate ligament in his left knee after suggesting the knee was merely sprained.

"He told me I was incompetent and was costing his team thousands of dollars," Kolb said. "Hundreds of thousands. Mr. Wirtz was like a madman. He even accused me of wanting Colorado to win. I don't need this."

Wirtz exploded when he discovered Kolb had allowed Colorado team physician Andrew Parker to perform arthroscopic surgery on Zhamnov without informing the Blackhawks. Kolb admitted he had done so, because Parker was licensed to practice in Colorado and he was not. Zhamnov needed the surgery because of a bloody ligament which, some time before the procedure, became infected. Kolb refused to take responsibility for the infection.

Asked about Kolb's bizarre departure, coach Craig Hartsburg sided with his boss. "I'm happy he's gone," he said.

Graham Out, Molleken In and Out

ON February 22, 1999, the Blackhawks made yet another coaching change: Dirk Graham was out, Lorne Molleken in. Unlike Graham, Molleken was not well known in NHL circles, but the 42-year-old Regina native had paid his dues coaching at the Junior and minor pro levels before joining the Blackhawks as an assistant coach.

Graham, a fan favorite as a player and team captain, was

ousted as coach just 59 games into the 1998–99 season. General manager Bob Murray took the blame for initially touting Graham for the job despite his lack of experience as a head coach.

Graham said, "I don't feel Bob Murray put me in a difficult spot. I'm glad I took the job, glad I had the opportunity. I just feel badly for the way it turned out."

The Hawks thought enough of Graham to keep him within the organization as a pro scout, the same role he'd handled well before accepting the coaching chores.

Molleken finished out the 1998–99 season on a high, but ran into a hornet's nest when the new season got under way. He wasn't at all pleased with the Hawks' slow start and bristled at charges he was handling the dirtiest team on skates.

He received a rude welcome to the league after a preseason game in Washington. Capitals GM George McPhee, furious that the Hawks had iced a lineup made up of their toughest players, rushed all the way around the rink to vilify coach Molleken with some choice language. Then he threw a solid punch that blackened Lorne's eye. McPhee paid for his assault with a one-month suspension without pay.

When the whistle signaled the start of a new season, Molleken's men tied a club record with an eight-game winless streak (4 losses and 4 ties). After his first four games, Doug Gilmour, the team's $6 million man, was a minus-5 and had just one point — an assist. Wendel Clark completely lost his scoring touch and was allowed to buy out his contract, and equally unproductive Bob Probert, a shadow of his former self, was still on the roster.

Before the season became a complete disaster, the Hawks fired GM Bob Murray and demoted Molleken to an assistant coaching role. Bob Pulford, a longtime jack-of-all-trades in the Hawks organization, agreed to take over indefinitely as head coach and manager.

Strachan Calls Hawks
a Laughing Stock

AFTER the Hawks fired general manager Bob Murray and demoted coach Lorne Molleken, veteran hockey columnist Al Strachan of *The Toronto Sun* wrote that "the Blackhawks give the NHL something it hasn't had for years — a true laughing stock." Wrote Strachan:

Bob Pulford as coach and general manager? That makes a lot of sense, doesn't it? He would be in over his head in either position, and now he is taking on both of them.

Considering its locale, this latest shuffle is not a surprise. The Blackhawks have a history of repeating mistakes over and over. So it doesn't come as a shock they have made this mistake once again.

They make the same coaching mistakes in that they grab players off the ice and shove them behind the bench, then expect them to be able to compete against coaches who have been doing the job for a lifetime. You can go all the way back to Bill White for an example. Or Keith Magnuson, right up to Darryl Sutter, Craig Hartsburg and Dirk Graham. They also make the same general manager mistakes, namely bringing back Bob Pulford every time the mood strikes.

Pulford was the Hawks' GM from 1977–78 to 1989–90, during which time the Hawks won absolutely nothing. Mike Keenan came in for two years (as GM, four years as coach) and took the Hawks to the Stanley Cup final. Reaching the Cup final was such a stunning departure from the norm the Hawks had no choice — they immediately fired Keenan and replaced him with, who else, Pulford.

That meant five more years in the wilderness for the Hawks, after which Pulford retired. But this team can't even do a retirement properly. Pulford stayed in the building, sticking his fingers into all decisions, hanging around with owner Bill Wirtz and being a general pain in the posterior for everyone else in the organization.

As long as they are not running a team for which you have any affinity, Wirtz and Pulford are kind of fun, a throwback to the NHL's darkest days when fools like Harold Ballard were making a travesty of the Toronto Maple Leafs.

In fact, there is very little difference between the Hawks of today and the Leafs under Ballard. Changes are made on a whim. Coaches, preferably those with no experience, are shuffled in and out. Public relations are considered to be too expensive to warrant any attention whatsoever. All decisions are made for financial reasons, without the slightest concern for on-ice success. Television exposure is seen as something that does more harm than good.

On Tuesday, when Pulford growled his way through what will probably be the only news conference of his tenure, he explained he had taken the job in the hopes he could fill some of the empty seats in the building. Nothing about playing better. Nothing about winning. Just sell more tickets.

If it weren't such a laughable situation, it would be pathetic.

Mike Smith's Biggest Challenge

IF Mike Smith thought it was tough making winners of the Winnipeg Jets and Toronto Maple Leafs, he must have asked himself how he could make chicken salad out of chicken droppings when he agreed to a job with the Chicago Blackhawks, who were floundering in last place in the Western Conference.

On December 12, 1999, Smith was named the Hawks' manager of hockey operations. He'd played a similar role with the Leafs, reporting to club president and GM Ken Dryden. Smith kept pushing Dryden to name him general manager, but Dryden procrastinated, preferring to keep the title for himself. It was only after Smith left that Dryden decided to give up the GM position, which was taken by team coach Pat Quinn. Quinn wisely decided to protect his own role in the organization by assuming the dual job of coach and GM.

Smith's first NHL management job was with Winnipeg in 1988–89, and controversy dogged him there, too. He replaced John Ferguson as the man in charge, and Fergie continues to hold a grudge against Smith, claiming that Smith bad-mouthed him to the team's owner.

I asked Ferguson one day if all the feuds from the past — those brawls he ignited with all the NHL's tough guys — were long forgotten. He said they were. "There's only one guy I hate now. That's Mike Smith."

The 54-year-old Smith understands his new job also represents his biggest challenge. Not only is he charged with improving a pathetic Blackhawk team, but he'll also have his hands full satisfying the Chicago management committee composed of Bob Pulford, Bill Wirtz, Peter Wirtz, Rocky Wirtz, and associate coach Lorne Molleken. It will be monitoring his every move.

"I am the manager," he insists. "I wouldn't have taken this job if I wasn't going to be in charge. I have been assured that I can make the appropriate changes."

It's a given that Smith is not happy with what he has seen so far, so look for him to try to make plenty of changes. But as one former Blackhawk employee told Mike Brophy of *The Hockey News*, "If Smith thinks he'll have autonomy there, he's dreaming."

THE BLACKHAWKS
THROUGH THE YEARS

1926–27 CHICAGO IS GRANTED AN NHL FRANCHISE on September 25, 1926. Major Frederic McLaughlin purchases the Portland Rosebuds' players for $150,000, transports them to Chicago, and names the team the Blackhawks in honor of a field gun battalion he commanded during World War I. Pete Muldoon is named first coach. The team plays its home games in the 6,000-seat Chicago Coliseum. The Hawks win their first home game 4–1 over Toronto St. Pats. They lead all teams in scoring with 115 goals. They finish third in the five-team American Division and are eliminated by Boston in the first playoff round.

1927–28 BARNEY STANLEY REPLACES MULDOON AS coach. The Blackhawks win only 7 games in the 1927–28 season, give up a league-high 134 goals, and finish fifth in the American Division. In an unsuccessful attempt to turn the club around, coach Stanley suits up for a game before being fired. He is replaced by Hugh Lehman, who had quit as Chicago's goaltender earlier in the season.

1928–29 HERB GARDINER IS NAMED COACH. The Blackhawks again win only 7 games. They play 8 straight games without scoring a goal, score only 33 all season, and are shut out 20 times. Vic Ripley leads the team in scoring with 11 goals and 2 assists. On March 28, 1929, Chicago Stadium opens, hosting a boxing match between lightweight champion Tommy Loughran and challenger Mickey Walker. Charlie Gardiner establishes himself as one of the league's best goaltenders by posting a 1.85 goals-against average in 44 games.

1929-30 TOM SHAUGHNESSY, AN ATTORNEY, is hired to coach the Hawks. He quits in midseason to return to his law practice and is replaced by Bill Tobin. On December 15, the Hawks play their first game at Chicago Stadium and defeat Pittsburgh 3–1. On March 13, the Blackhawks defeat the Boston Bruins, ending the Bruins' record-tying undefeated streak at 17 games. Chicago improves by 25 points over the previous season, finishes in second place in the American Division with a 21–18–5 record. The Montreal Canadiens defeat the Blackhawks in the first round of NHL playoffs, winning the two-game, total-goals series 3–2.

1930–31 DICK IRVIN REPLACES BILL TOBIN BEHIND the Chicago bench. Charlie Gardiner allows only 78 goals in 44 games. The Blackhawks end the season at 24–17–3, finish in second place in the American Division behind the Boston Bruins. The Hawks make it to the Stanley Cup finals for the first time, but lose to the Canadiens in five games.

1931–32 JAMES NORRIS TAKES SOME CONTROL OF Chicago Stadium after Major McLaughlin decides not to bid for it. McLaughlin unsuccessfully tries to implement a rule that teams be penalized for icing the puck while at even strength. John Gottselig, the NHL's first Russian-born player, leads team in goals (13) and points (28). Dick Irvin is fired as coach and snapped up by Toronto. He leads the Leafs to a playoff victory over the Hawks and takes Toronto to the Stanley Cup. Charlie Gardiner wins Chicago's first major individual award, taking the Vezina Trophy as the league's best goaltender.

1932–33 ON DECEMBER 18, CHICAGO BEARS defeat Portsmouth 9–0 in the first NFL championship game, played indoors (because of a blizzard) at the Stadium. Godfrey Matheson, a high school teacher, takes over as Hawks coach, but he's soon replaced by Emil Iverson. On January 5, McLaughlin resigns as team governor, only to reinstate himself in early February. Iverson is replaced as coach by Tommy Gorman, whose team finishes in last place in the four-team American Division after posting a 16–20–12 record. The Hawks forfeit a game — the first in NHL history — when players refuse to take the ice after a referee ejects coach Gorman.

1933–34 THE HAWKS FINISH THE SEASON IN
second place in the American Division with a 20–17–11 record. Charlie Gardiner wins the Vezina Trophy on the strength of a 1.63 goals-against average. The Blackhawks win their first-ever Stanley Cup when Harold "Mush" March scores against Detroit after 30:05 of overtime in game four of the finals. Two months after the Stanley Cup victory, Charlie Gardiner, 29, enters a Winnipeg hospital for an operation and dies on the table from a massive brain tumor.

1934–35 CLEM LOUGHLIN IS CHICAGO'S NEW
coach, replacing Tommy Gorman. Goalie Lorne Chabot, Howie Morenz, and Marty Burke are acquired from the Montreal Canadiens in a major trade. Chabot wins the Vezina Trophy in his first season with the Hawks. Morenz scores only 8 goals in 48 games. Chicago finishes with a 26–17–5 record for second place in their division, but falls to the Montreal Maroons in the first round of playoffs.

1935–36 LORNE CHABOT IS INJURED AND MIKE
Karakas, an American-born goaltender, is given a chance. He is voted the league's top rookie. Morenz is traded to the New York Rangers and Chabot is sold to a minor-league team in Pittsburgh. He refuses to report and winds up with the Maroons. With a record of 21–19–8, the Hawks finish the season in third place in their division but lose to the New York Americans 7–5 in a two-game, total-goals playoff series. Doc Romnes wins the Lady Byng Trophy.

1936–37 CLEM LOUGHLIN RETURNS FOR HIS THIRD season behind the bench. In a January game at Montreal, Earl Seibert collides with the Habs' Howie Morenz, who suffers a broken leg. Thirty-nine days later, Morenz dies in hospital. In the last five games of the season, McLaughlin ices a starting lineup of American-born players. In five games, his team is 1–4, is outscored 27–13, and the experiment is abandoned. The Blackhawks finish in last place with a 14–27–7 record.

1937–38 BILL STEWART, A MAJOR-LEAGUE BASEBALL umpire and NHL referee, is hired as coach. The Blackhawks win only 14 games but finish third in their division. They oust the Canadiens and then the Americans in the opening rounds of the playoffs. Then they shock the hockey world, defeating the Toronto Maple Leafs 3 games to 1 in the finals to win their second Stanley Cup in five seasons. John Gottselig finishes the playoffs with 5 goals and 8 points in 10 games. Carl "Cully" Dahlstrom wins the Calder Trophy as best rookie.

1938–39 ON OPENING NIGHT AT THE STADIUM, Bill Stewart is presented with the Stanley Cup before 16,000 fans. Halfway through the season he is fired and replaced by player-coach Paul Thompson. The Hawks score only 91 goals and finish in last place in the revamped seven-team league with a 12–28–8 record.

1939-40 THE HAWKS BECOME A TWO-GOALIE TEAM when Paul Goodman is called up to share netminding chores with Mike Karakas. Karakas is later ordered to the minors, refuses to report, and the league arranges for him to play with the Canadiens. The Blackhawks finish the regular season with a much-improved 23–19–6 record, good for fourth place. The Hawks fly to Toronto — becoming the first NHL team to charter an aircraft — for the opening playoff round. The Hawks lose to the Leafs 2–0 in the best-of-three series.

1940–41 PAUL THOMPSON IS BACK AS COACH. Sam LoPresti is brought in to share goaltending chores with Paul Goodman. Max Bentley is signed and joins his brother Doug. Rookie Max scores 7 goals; Doug scores 8. On March 16, 1941, coach Paul Thompson pulls goaltender LoPresti in a game against the Toronto Maple Leafs. The Hawks claim it's a hockey "first." On March 4, LoPresti stops a record 80 of 83 shots, in a losing effort against the Bruins. The Blackhawks eliminate the Canadiens in the first round of playoffs, then lose to Detroit in the second round.

1941–42 THE BLACKHAWKS SIGN FUTURE STAR Bill Mosienko, along with rookies Alex Kaleta and George Johnson. On New Year's night, the Detroit Red Wings defeat the Blackhawks 3–0. The game features a fight between Hawk Earl Seibert and the Wings' Jimmy Orlando, who is knocked down twice before he can remove his gloves. When Orlando gets his gloves off, Seibert knocks him to the ice twice more. The Blackhawks finish fourth with a 22–23–3 record. Bill Thoms leads the team in points with 45 while rookie Mosienko, called up from Kansas City, collects 14 points in 12 games. The Bruins eliminate the Hawks 2 games to 1 in the first playoff round.

1942–43 WHEN GOALIE SAM LOPRESTI LEAVES FOR military service, the Hawks borrow Bert Gardiner from the Canadiens. Chicago boasts an all-Bentley line of brothers Reg, Doug, and Max. Max Bentley scores 7 points (4 goals, 3 assists) in a 10–1 thrashing of the New York Rangers. Chicago finishes fifth and misses the playoffs. Doug Bentley wins the NHL scoring title with 73 points in 50 games. Brother Max finishes third with 70 points and draws only one minor penalty in 47 games. He captures the Lady Byng Trophy.

1943–44 ON FEBRUARY 20, THE HAWKS AND THE Toronto Maple Leafs play a so-called "perfect game" at the Stadium. The game ends in a scoreless tie with no penalties called.

Doug Bentley finishes second in NHL scoring with 38 goals and 39 assists for 77 points. Chicago finishes fourth with a 22–23–5 record. The Hawks defeat the Red Wings 4 games to 1 in the first round of playoffs, then lose to the Canadiens in four straight games. Clint Smith is presented with the Lady Byng Trophy.

1944–45 ON OCTOBER 29, AFTER THE HAWKS FALL 11–5 to the Toronto Maple Leafs, coach Paul Thompson is fired and replaced by former player John Gottselig. On December 17, hockey mourns the loss of Major Frederic McLaughlin, the Blackhawks' first owner. Newly appointed club president Bill Tobin trades Earl Seibert to Detroit for Don Grosso, Cully Simon, and Byron McDonald. Chicago ends the season one point out of last place with a 13–30–7 record. Bill Mosienko and Clint Smith finish in a tie for club scoring with 54 points in 50 games. Both finish the season penalty-free and Mosienko is awarded the Lady Byng Trophy.

1945–46 THE FAMOUS PONY LINE IS REUNITED AS Max Bentley returns from military service to join brother Doug and Bill Mosienko. On October 24, Chicago opens at Boston — the earliest opener in league history. On January 12 in a 4–3 loss at Boston Garden, Hawk players Joe Cooper, Reg Hamilton, John Mariucci, and trainer Ed Froelich are arrested and charged with assault and battery after a melee near the Chicago bench. The charges are later dismissed. The Hawks finish with a 23–20–7 record, good enough for third place. Despite a late-season injury, Max Bentley wins the scoring title with 61 points and is awarded the Hart Trophy as league MVP. The Hawks bow to the Canadiens in the first round of the playoffs, losing four straight games.

1946–47 IN THE OFF-SEASON, GOALTENDER Paul Bibeault is picked up from Montreal to replace the floundering Mike Karakas. On November 30, the Leafs humiliate the Hawks 11–0. February 9 marks the debut of Emile "The Cat" Francis in goal, and more than 20,000 fans see him help defeat Boston. Max Bentley wins the scoring crown by a single point over Maurice Richard (72 points to 71) in 60 games. The Hawks finish a disappointing season with a 19–37–4 record and sink into last place in the standings.

1947–48 PAUL BIBEAULT IS RETURNED TO Montreal and Emile Francis takes over in goal. Two days prior to the regular season, Bill Mosienko breaks his ankle in the All-Star Game. After losing their first 6 games, the Hawks trade league scoring champ Max Bentley and Cy Thomas to the Maple Leafs for Bob Goldham, Ernie Dickens, Gus Bodnar, Gaye Stewart, and Bud Poile. On November 12, classy veteran Roy Conacher comes out of retirement. President Bill Tobin fires coach Gottselig and replaces him with Charlie Conacher. The Hawks finish with a 20–34–6 record, in last place for the second straight year.

1948–49 THE HAWKS LOSE THEIR FIRST 4 GAMES before trading Bud Poile and George Gee to the Red Wings for center Jim Conacher, left winger Bep Guidolin, and defenseman Doug McCaig. On November 3, Chicago hosts the 2nd annual All-Star Game. The Mosienko-Bentley-Conacher line begins producing. Chicago signs rookie Bert Olmstead to a contract. Chicago finishes with a 21–31–8 record, and is out of the playoffs.

1949–50 THE HAWKS SIGN AGING GOALTENDER Frankie Brimsek and 20-year-old rookie Vic Stasiuk. Coach Charlie Conacher, irate after his team is whipped 9–2 in Detroit on February 8, punches Lew Walter, a writer with the Detroit *Times*. Walter wants Conacher arrested but is pacified by a written apology. The Hawks fail to qualify for the playoffs and finish in the league's cellar with a 22–38–10 record. Bert Olmstead scores 20 goals in his first full season.

1950–51 CHARLIE CONACHER RESIGNS AND IS replaced by former Red Wing Ebbie Goodfellow. President Bill Tobin engineers a nine-player swap with the Red Wings, sending goalie Jim Henry, defenseman Bob Goldham, forward Metro Prystai, and veteran Gaye Stewart to the Wings for goaltender Harry Lumley, defensemen "Black Jack" Stewart and Al Dewsbury, center Don Morrison, and left winger Pete Babando. The Hawks again finish last in the standings with a pitiful record of 13–47–10.

1951–52 FOR $75,000, THE HAWKS PURCHASE George Gee, Jim McFadden, Jim Peters, Clare Martin, Max McNab, and Clare Raglan from Detroit. On November 24, when goaltender Harry Lumley is injured, 45-year-old trainer Moe Roberts straps on the pads for 20 minutes and becomes the oldest player in NHL history. On January 17, Bill Mosienko picks up his 200th goal as the Hawks and Rangers skate to a 6–6 draw. On January 20, the Hawks try to attract fans with the first-ever Sunday matinee game. Bill Mosienko sets an NHL record with three goals in 21 seconds. Chicago's overall record is a dismal 17–44–9 resulting in the fifth last-place finish in six years.

1952–53 BILL TOBIN SELLS HIS CONTROLLING interest in the club to the owners of Chicago Stadium — James D. Norris and Arthur Wirtz. Coach Ebbie Goodfellow is fired and former Detroit center Sid Abel is brought in as playing coach. The Hawks trade Harry Lumley to the Leafs for center Cal Gardner, defenseman Gus Mortson, and 26-year-old goaltender Al Rollins.

1953–54 THE HAWKS ADD FORMER RED WINGS Larry Wilson, Lou Jankowski, and Larry Zeidel, ex–Bruin left winger Jack McIntyre, and rookie Murray Costello. With attendance in decline, the media begin to hint that a Hawk-less league of only five teams might be a wise move. The Hawks finish in last place with an atrocious 12–51–7 record, 37 points behind the fifth-place Rangers.

1954–55 COACH SID ABEL RESIGNS AND FORMER
Ranger defenseman Frank Eddolls replaces him. The Wirtz-Norris-Ivan triumvirate begins to clean house. Larry Zeidel, George Gee, and Jim McFadden are cast aside, replaced by Harry Watson from Toronto, Metro Prystai from Detroit, and rookie right winger Ed Litzenberger from Montreal. Bill Mosienko comes out of retirement to aid the ailing franchise. Once again the Hawks endure a fruitless season and finish in last place with a record of 13–40–17. Litzenberger wins the Calder Trophy after scoring 16 goals and 24 assists in only 44 games.

1955–56 FRANK EDDOLLS IS DISMISSED AS COACH
and replaced by Dick Irvin. The Hawks count heavily on four recent additions: Ed Litzenberger, George "Red" Sullivan, Nick Mickoski, and John "Iron Man" Wilson. Wilson leads the club in goals scored with 24, Sullivan in points with 40. Rookie defenseman Pierre Pilote is brought up for 20 games and shows promise. The Hawks finish in last place again with a 19–39–12 record.

1956–57 WITH 64-YEAR-OLD COACH DICK IRVIN
suffering from bone cancer, general manager Tommy Ivan assumes coaching responsibilities as well. Leading scorer Red Sullivan is dealt to the Rangers for Wally Hergesheimer, who scores a mere 2 goals. Litzenberger triples his goal production of the previous season, finishing with 32 and a team-high 64 points. Pierre Pilote and rookie Elmer "Moose" Vasko become regulars on defense and Eric Nesterenko makes his Chicago debut. However, the Hawks fail to climb out of the league cellar.

1957–58 TOMMY IVAN ACQUIRES GOALTENDER Glenn Hall and "Terrible" Ted Lindsay from Detroit in exchange for Forbes Kennedy, Hank Bassen, and John Wilson. An 18-year-old rookie, Robert Marvin Hull, later to be known as The Golden Jet, makes a splendid debut. In midseason, Ivan engineers an eight-player deal with Detroit, sending Hector Lalonde, Jack McIntyre, Nick Mickoski, and Bob Bailey to the Wings for Bill Dineen, Earl Reibel, Lorne Ferguson, and Billy Dea. Ivan brings in a new coach, Rudy Pilous, but the Hawks finish fifth with a 24–39-7 record. Bobby Hull collects 47 points, 11 more than Leaf rookie Frank Mahovlich, who wins the Calder.

1958–59 THE HAWKS ACQUIRE THREE PROVEN defensemen: Al Arbour from Detroit, Jack Evans from the Rangers, and Dollard St. Laurent from Montreal. Tod Sloan and Earl Balfour are acquired from the Leafs. Despite a stronger lineup, the Hawks have trouble at the box office and, after the first 15 home games, attract 40,000 fewer fans than the previous season. Rookie Stan Mikita plays 3 games in midseason but injures his shoulder and returns to Junior hockey. The Hawks finish with a 28–29–13 record, good enough for third place.

1959-60 THE HAWKS PRY MURRAY BALFOUR AWAY from Montreal and sign rookie Red Hay, a college player, to a contract. Despite these additions, the Hawks go 14 games without a win before defeating Detroit 5–3 on November 15. At the halfway mark, the club is a woeful 10–18–8. On January 19, Ed Litzenberger is seriously injured, and his wife killed, in an auto accident. Bobby Hull finishes a point ahead of Boston's Bronco Horvath to win the scoring title (81–80) while Bill Hay, second in team scoring with 55 points, captures the Calder. Jacques Plante edges out Glenn Hall for the Vezina. A third-place finish (28–29–13) pits Chicago against Montreal in the semifinals.

1960–61 TED LINDSAY RETIRES. COACH PILOUS

counts heavily on the Million-Dollar Line of Bobby Hull, Murray Balfour, and Bill Hay. The Hawks deal with Montreal for Ab McDonald, who becomes a perfect fit with Stan Mikita and Ken Wharram. Reggie Fleming, also acquired from Montreal, becomes the club's tough guy. The Hawks finish with a 29–24–17 record, good enough for third place and another playoff matchup with Montreal, winners of five consecutive Stanley Cups. The Hawks stun the Habs with a 4-games-to-2 victory in the first round, and follow up with their first Stanley Cup victory in 23 years over Detroit.

1961–62 THE HAWKS OBTAIN DEFENSEMAN Bob

Turner from Montreal. Tod Sloan and Earl Balfour are released and Ed Litzenberger is shipped to Detroit in a trade for Gerry Melnyk and Brian Smith. Goalie Glenn Hall plays in his 500th consecutive game (including playoffs) and is rewarded by team owner Jim Norris with a new car. Bobby Hull scores his 50th goal in the final game and captures the Art Ross Trophy with 84 points. The Hawks finish in third place, then upset Montreal 4 games to 2 in the semifinals. But they lose in the finals by the same margin to Toronto.

1962–63 OWNER JIM NORRIS MAKES A STUNNING

offer to Toronto — $1 million for Frank Mahovlich. The Leafs ultimately reject the offer. Glenn Hall's consecutive game streak comes to an end when a pinched nerve in his back forces him out of regular-season game 503. On January 27, Hab goalie Jacques Plante demands a measurement of the Chicago goal nets and they are found to be two inches shorter than regulation. The Hawks finish one point behind first-place Toronto in the standings. The Hawks are eliminated by Detroit in 6 games in the semifinals.

1963–64 RUDY PILOUS IS DISMISSED AS COACH and replaced by Billy Reay. Defensemen Bob Turner and Jack Evans are replaced and Phil Esposito is brought up from the minors. Chicago holds a 5-point lead over Montreal at the halfway mark with a 20–8–7 record. The Hawks finish second, one point behind Montreal. The Hawks lose a 7-game series to Detroit in the first playoff round.

1964–65 THREE ROOKIES, DENNIS HULL, Doug Jarrett, and Fred Stanfield join the Hawks. Tommy Ivan ships Ab McDonald and Reg Fleming to Boston for Doug Mohns. Stan Mikita captures another scoring title with 87 points. Pierre Pilote wins his third consecutive Norris, and Bobby Hull is awarded the Hart and Lady Byng trophies. The Hawks advance to the Stanley Cup finals after a 7-game series with Detroit.

1965–66 TOMMY IVAN ADDS PROMISING ROOKIE Ken Hodge to the Chicago lineup and snares defenseman Pat Stapleton in the Intra-League Draft from Toronto. Bobby Hull and Stan Mikita begin using sticks with "banana" blades. On February 25, Chicago mourns the death of James D. Norris, co-owner of the Hawks. Bobby Hull breaks the 50-goal plateau with his 51st on March 12 versus New York's Cesare Maniago. He finishes with 54 goals and 97 points — both NHL records. He wins the Art Ross and Hart trophies. The Hawks finish second, 8 points behind Montreal, but are eliminated by fourth-place Detroit in 6 games in the first round of the playoffs.

1966–67 ELMER VASKO RETIRES. THE HAWKS SCORE a league-record 264 goals with Bobby Hull contributing 52. Stan Mikita wins the Art Ross Trophy for the third time and also captures the Lady Byng and Hart trophies. Chicago's 41–17–12 record earns them first place with a 17-point bulge over second-place Montreal. But a fired-up Toronto Maple Leafs squad eliminates the Hawks in the semifinals, 4 games to 2, denying Chicago a Stanley Cup berth in the final season of the "Original Six."

1967–68 IN THE NHL'S FIRST-EVER expansion draft, the Hawks lose goalie Glenn Hall to St. Louis, and Lou Angotti, John Miszuk, and Ed Van Impe to Philadelphia. Hawk fans groan when Tommy Ivan deals Phil Esposito, Ken Hodge, and Fred Stanfield to Boston for Gilles Marotte, Pit Martin, and goalie Jack Norris. Stan Mikita leads the league in scoring with 87 points and once again captures three major awards — the Ross, Lady Byng, and Hart trophies. The Hawks finish in fourth place in the East Division, eliminate the Rangers in the quarterfinals, but are ousted by Montreal in the semis.

1968–69 THE HAWKS TRADE 13-YEAR VETERAN Pierre Pilote to Toronto for Jim Pappin. They score their biggest-ever shutout — a 12–0 thumping of Philadelphia — on January 30. Bobby Hull scores 58 goals and collects 107 points, but is overshadowed by former teammate Phil Esposito, who amasses a record 126 points to win the scoring crown. The Hawks slide all the way to the East Division basement with a 34–33–9 record and miss the playoffs.

1969–70 TOMMY IVAN ACQUIRES THE RIGHTS TO defenseman Bill White from Los Angeles. Lou Angotti is re-acquired from Pittsburgh. Ken Wharram retires. The Hawks sign ex-college stars Keith Magnuson and Cliff Koroll. Bobby Hull scores his 500th career goal against New York on February 21. Esposito records his 15th shutout of the season — a modern-day record — on March 29. The Hawks finish in a dead heat with Boston for first place in the East with 99 points, but are awarded the title because they have 5 more wins. Chicago eliminates the Red Wings in four straight games in the quarterfinals, then falls in four straight to Boston in the semifinals.

1970–71 CHICAGO IS THE ONLY MEMBER OF THE Original Six to be moved to the West Division. Rookies Dan Maloney and Jerry Korab join the Hawks, who dominate their division and end the campaign with 107 points and a 49–20–9 record. In the playoffs, the Hawks eliminate Philadelphia in four games and oust the Rangers in a seven-game series. The Hawks loses a 3–2 heartbreaker at the Stadium in the deciding match against the Habs.

1971–72 THE SEASON OPENS AMID RUMORS A NEW league — the World Hockey Association — is on the horizon. Despite some roster juggling, the Hawks finish with a 46–17–15 record and another first-place finish in the West Division. Tony Esposito teams with backup Gary Smith to win the Vezina. Bobby Hull scores his final regular-season goal as a Blackhawk (his 604th) on April 2 against Detroit. In the playoffs, the Hawks eliminate Pittsburgh in four games, then fall in four games to the New York Rangers.

1972–73 THE WORLD HOCKEY ASSOCIATION arrives and Bobby Hull leaves Chicago to sign a million-dollar contract with the Winnipeg Jets, lending the new circuit instant credibility. The Hawks win the West Division title with 93 points, 8 more than Philadelphia. They oust St. Louis in five games in the quarterfinals, then eliminate the Rangers, also in five games. Montreal wins the Cup over the Hawks.

1973–74 THE CHICAGO COUGARS OF THE WHA lure Pat Stapleton and Ralph Backstrom away from the Hawks with lucrative contracts. Tommy Ivan deals with Vancouver for Dale Tallon, who becomes a blueline fixture. The Hawks finish with a 41–14–23 record, 7 points behind the Philadelphia Flyers in the West Division. In the playoffs, the Hawks push Los Angeles aside in five games but are eliminated in the second round, losing to Boston in six games.

1974–75 TWO NEW FRANCHISES, WASHINGTON and Kansas City, join the NHL. The league is realigned, and Chicago is placed in the Smythe Division of the Campbell Conference. Tommy Ivan trades Len Frig to California for Ivan Boldirev, who contributes 67 points. The Hawks finish third in the weak Smythe Division, seventh-worst overall. They upset Boston in the three-game preliminary-round playoff series, then fall to Buffalo in five in the quarterfinals.

1975–76 THE HAWKS TRADE JIM PAPPIN TO California for Joey Johnston. On October 29, the Hawks embark on a 15-game undefeated streak. They finish with a record of 32–30–18, good enough for first place in the Smythe Division, but they manage only three goals in four quarterfinal playoff games and are swept aside by Montreal.

1976–77 ON JUNE 24 THE HAWKS ANNOUNCE THE signing of free-agent superstar Bobby Orr. They add Jim Harrison, a refugee from the WHA. After an 11-game winless streak, coach Billy Reay is fired and replaced by Bill White. Ivan Boldirev leads the team in scoring with 62 points. Orr plays in 20 games and scores 4 goals. The Hawks finish third in the Smythe Division with a 26–43–11 record and are swept in the best-of-three preliminary playoff round by the New York Islanders.

1977–78 BOB PULFORD IS HIRED AS HEAD COACH and general manager. Dennis Hull is sent to Detroit. Rookie Doug Wilson becomes a regular on defense. Mike O'Connell becomes the first Chicago-born player to skate as a Hawk. Ivan Boldirev leads the team in scoring with 80 points. Orr's ailing knees keep him sidelined for the entire season. Chicago earns first place in the Smythe Division with a mediocre 32–29–19 record. The Hawks lose to Boston in four straight games in the Stanley Cup quarterfinals.

1978–79 GOALIE ED JOHNSTON RETIRES. ORR PLAYS in 6 games, scores 2 goals before retiring in November. Chicago finishes first in the weak Smythe Division with a 29–36–15 record. In their quarterfinal series against the Islanders, the Hawks score a mere three goals and are ousted in four straight games.

1979–80 BOB PULFORD FOCUSES ON MANAGING the Hawks and signs Eddie Johnston as coach. Darryl Sutter and Keith Brown make their Chicago debuts. Pulford acquires Terry Ruskowski and Rich Preston from Winnipeg. Cliff Koroll, Stan Mikita, and Keith Magnuson struggle through one more season but Magnuson's wonky knee forces him into retirement before Christmas. With 87 points, the Hawks capture the Smythe Division title. They oust St. Louis in three straight games in the first round but are eliminated in four straight by Buffalo in the quarterfinals.

1980–81 THE HAWKS RETIRE THE FIRST JERSEY IN team history, Stan Mikita's Number 21. Keith Magnuson takes over from Ed Johnston as Blackhawk coach. Goalie Murray Bannerman, acquired from Vancouver in 1978, relieves Tony Esposito in 15 games. Denis Savard, Chicago's top draft pick (third overall), enjoys a dazzling rookie season with 28 goals and 75 points. The Hawks finish second in the Smythe Division but are eliminated in the preliminary round by Calgary in three straight games.

1981–82 THE NHL IS AGAIN REALIGNED, AND THE Hawks are placed in the Norris Division. In midseason, as the Hawks slump, Bob Pulford replaces Keith Magnuson as coach "for a few games." Magnuson returns, but resigns after his first game back. Denis Savard leads the team in scoring with 119 points. The Hawks finish fourth in the Norris Division with a

30–38–12 record but defeat Minnesota and St. Louis in the play-offs. The Vancouver Canucks end Chicago's season in the next round with an easy 4-games-to-1 victory.

1982–83 ORVAL TESSIER IS COACH. Hawks Denis Cyr, Denis Savard's linemate in Junior, is acquired and scores 7 goals in 41 games. Tony Tanti is traded to Vancouver for Curt Fraser. Steve Larmer enjoys a sensational rookie season (43 goals, 47 assists) and wins the Calder Trophy. Denis Savard leads the team in scoring with 121 points. Al Secord scores 54 goals. The Hawks top the Norris Division with a 47–23–10 record and oust the Blues in the first round, Minnesota in the second. Tessier wins the Jack Adams Trophy as NHL coach of the year. The Oilers eliminate Chicago in four.

1983–84 CHICAGO DRAFTS 18-YEAR-OLD CZECH goalie Dominik Hasek 207th overall. On July 21, Arthur Wirtz dies. Bobby Hull's number, 9, is retired. Tom Lysiak receives a 20-game suspension, the second-longest in NHL history, for knocking down a linesman. The Hawks finish with a dismal record (30–42–8) and finish fourth in the Norris Division. They bow to Minnesota in five games in the first playoff round.

1984–85 ROGER NEILSON IS HIRED AS ASSISTANT coach. Blackhawks draft Chicago-born Ed Olczyk. In midseason Orval Tessier is fired and Bob Pulford decides to coach. The Hawks finish 38–35–7 for second place in the Norris. They eliminate Detroit in three straight games but need six to oust the Minnesota North Stars. In the conference finals against the Oilers, the Hawks lose in six.

1985–86 GOALIE BOB SAUVE IS ACQUIRED FROM Buffalo. Denis Savard leads the club in scoring with 116 points. The Hawks finish first in the Norris Division with a 39–33–8

record, but are swept by Toronto in a best-of-five first-round playoff series. Troy Murray wins the Frank Selke Trophy as the NHL's best defensive forward.

1986–87 THE HAWKS SELECT EVERETT SANIPASS, A full-blooded Mi'kmaq Indian, with their first selection in the NHL draft. They re-acquire Rich Preston from the Devils and sign free-agent defenseman Gary Nylund. Tom Lysiak retires. Al Secord scores 4 goals in 8:24 to set a club record. The Hawks finish third in the Norris Division and fall to Detroit in four straight games in the first round of playoffs.

1987–88 BOB MURDOCH IS SIGNED AS THE NEW Chicago coach. The Hawks draft goalie Jimmy Waite in the first round (8th overall) and sign free-agent goalies Bob Mason and Ed Belfour. They trade Al Secord and Ed Olczyk to Toronto for Steve Thomas, Rick Vaive, and Bob McGill. The Hawks lose 12–0 to Detroit, the most one-sided defeat in team history. The Hawks finish third in the Norris Division, then lose four of five games to St. Louis in the first playoff round.

1988–89 THE HAWKS DRAFT JEREMY ROENICK (8th overall). Mike Keenan signs as new Chicago coach. The Hawks retire the jerseys of Glenn Hall (Number 1) and Tony Esposito (Number 35). Steve Larmer plays in his 510th consecutive game — a club record. They secure a playoff berth with an overtime goal in the final game of the season. The Hawks oust the Red Wings from the playoffs in six games. They follow up with a 4–1 series victory over St. Louis before losing 4–1 to Calgary in the Campbell Conference finals.

1989–90 THE HAWKS DRAFT A TRIO OF BIG defensemen — Adam Bennett, Michael Speer, and Bob Kellogg — with their first three choices. Of the three, only Bennett ever plays for

the Hawks (21 career games, 2 points). Al Secord rejoins Chicago after two seasons in Toronto and Philadelphia. During a game, Calgary's Theo Fleury (5'5") calls Hawk goalie Alain Chevrier (5'8") a "sawed-off little runt." Denis Savard becomes the 26th NHL player to reach the 1,000-point plateau. The Hawks acquire Michel Goulet, 29, from Quebec. Bob Murray plays in his 1,000th game — all of them as a Hawk. Chicago finishes first in the Norris Division and eliminates Minnesota in seven games in the first playoff round. The Blackhawks oust St. Louis in seven games, then fall to Edmonton in six games in the Campbell Conference finals.

1990–91 DUANE SUTTER RETIRES. THE HAWKS trade
Denis Savard to Montreal for Chris Chelios and a second-round draft choice. Soviet legend Vladislav Tretiak signs on as goaltending coach and scout. Dominik Hasek is called up to join Ed Belfour, Jacques Cloutier, and Greg Millen on the Chicago goaltending roster. Jeremy Roenick excels in the All-Star Game, played at Chicago. Steve Larmer plays in his 700th consecutive game. The Hawks clinch a playoff spot for the 22nd consecutive season. Ed Belfour wins 43 games, and the Hawks win a club-record 49 games and the President's Trophy (for finishing first overall). They are upset by Minnesota in the first round of the playoffs. Ed Belfour wins the Vezina, the Jennings, and the Calder trophies. Dirk Graham wins the Selke Trophy.

1991–92 THE HAWKS TRADE DAVE MANSON TO
Edmonton in return for Steve Smith. John Tonelli plays in his 1,000th game. Dominik Hasek becomes Ed Belfour's backup. Michel Goulet scores his 500th career goal. The Hawks sign Igor Kravchuk, a star with Russia's Central Red Army team. Jeremy Roenick has his first 50-goal season. Ground is broken for the United Center. After a brief players strike, the Hawks roar into the playoffs, disposing of St. Louis (six games), Detroit (four games), and Edmonton (four games). They win a team-record 11 straight playoff games but lose to Pittsburgh, 4–0, in the Stanley Cup finals.

1992–93 DARRYL SUTTER IS NAMED HEAD COACH of the Blackhawks. Keenan is offered a contract extension as GM but is fired when he complains about not having the right to negotiate player contracts. Dominik Hasek is traded to Buffalo for goalie Stephane Beauregard and future considerations. The Hawks play exhibition games in England against Montreal. Pulford trades Igor Kravchuk and Dean McAmmond to Edmonton for Joe Murphy. The Hawks win their division, clinching a play-off berth for the 24th consecutive season. They lose to the Blues, 4–0, in the first round of playoffs. Ed Belfour wins his second Vezina Trophy, as well as the Jennings Trophy. Chelios wins the Norris Trophy.

1993–94 ERIC DAZE IS DRAFTED 90TH OVERALL. Jimmy Waite is traded to San Jose. The Hawks play their final season at Chicago Stadium. Chris Chelios sets two club records for penalties and ties a third. Pulford trades Steve Larmer and Bryan Marchment to Hartford for Patrick Poulin and Eric Weinrich. Hartford immediately deals Larmer to the New York Rangers. Prior to the playoffs, Steve Smith breaks his leg and Eric Weinrich breaks his jaw. The Hawks acquire Tony Amonte from the Rangers. Michel Goulet suffers a severe concussion, and is out for season. Anthem singer Wayne Messmer is shot in the throat during a robbery attempt. The Hawks are shut out three times in the first playoff round, which they lose to Toronto.

1994–95 MICHEL GOULET FAILS HIS PRESEASON physical because of a severe concussion suffered March 16, 1994, and retires with 548 career goals. Free agents Bob Probert and Bernie Nicholls join the Hawks. Probert is ruled ineligible to play until 1995–96. A collective-bargaining impasse leads to a lockout of NHL players. Chris Chelios makes controversial comments, relating to the lockout, about NHL commissioner Gary Bettman. Hawks begin play in the $175 million United Center. The Hawks re-acquire Denis Savard from Tampa Bay. Wayne Messmer returns to sing the anthems at the first game, but he will no longer be allowed to sing at Hawk games because he has taken an executive job with the Chicago Wolves of the IHL. Joe Murphy scores the first goal at the new arena. Denis Savard leads the Hawks to a first-round playoff win over Toronto. They go on to sweep Vancouver, winning three of the four games in overtime. Goalie Ed Belfour is sensational in Chicago's loss to Detroit in Western Conference finals. Craig Hartsburg succeeds Darryl Sutter as coach.

1995–96 TROUBLED WINGER BOB PROBERT PLAYS

his first game as a Hawk. Bill Wirtz suffers mild heart seizure. The Hawks sign Keith Tkachuk to a $17.2 million offer sheet, but Winnipeg matches the offer and Tkachuk stays with the Jets. Rookie Eric Daze impresses, scoring 30 goals. Denis Savard moves into 15th place on the all-time scoring list with 1,284 points. A reunion of the 1961 Cup champions brings 15 of 18 surviving players to a game in March. The Hawks set an NHL record by averaging 20,000 fans per game. They sweep the Calgary Flames in the first round of the playoffs, then lose to the Colorado Avalanche in six games in round two. Chris Chelios wins his third Norris Trophy (his second with Chicago). Jeremy Roenick is traded to Phoenix for Alexei Zhamnov, Craig Mills, and a first-round draft choice in 1997.

1996–97 THE HAWKS FAIL TO SELL OUT THE United

Center for their first seven home games. Arthur Michael Wirtz, Jr., the Hawks' executive vice president, dies of cancer. Bob Pulford gives Chris Chelios, 34, a contract extension and says, "He'll end his career in Chicago." Pulford trades goalie Ed Belfour to San Jose for Ulf Dahlen, Michal Sykora, and Chris Terreri. The Hawks finish eighth in the Western Conference. Team physician Dr. Louis Kolb resigns amid accusations by owner Bill Wirtz that he mistreated Hawk players. The Hawks are eliminated by Colorado in six games as the power play scores only one goal in 27 chances.

1997–98 DENIS SAVARD AND STEVE SMITH RETIRE prior to the season. Savard joins the Hawks as an assistant coach. Chris Chelios expresses surprise when *The Hockey News* names him one of the top 50 NHL players of all time. Chris Chelios, Gary Suter, Keith Carney, and Tony Amonte join Team USA for the Nagano Olympics. Owner Wirtz promises changes after the Hawks miss the playoffs for the first time in 29 years.

1998–99 THE HAWKS SIGN FREE AGENT Doug Gilmour, reacquire Ed Olczyk, and add backup goalie Mark Fitzpatrick after dealing Chris Terreri to New Jersey. Former Hawk Elmer "Moose" Vasko dies of cancer. Roy Conacher is elected to the Hockey Hall of Fame. Paul Coffey is traded to the Carolina Hurricanes for Nelson Emerson. Bob Probert scores the last NHL goal at Maple Leaf Gardens. Chris Chelios is dealt to Detroit for Anders Eriksson and two first-round picks. With the Hawks 19 games below .500, Dirk Graham is fired and replaced by Lorne Molleken. The Hawks go 8–1–2 in their final 11 games but miss the playoffs for the second straight season.

1999–2000 Lorne Mollekin is sucker-punched by Washington GM George McPhee during a pre-season game. The Hawks' 0-6-3-1 start at home breaks a 63-year-old club record. Holdout Boris Mironov signs a three-year $9.6-million contract. Owner Bill Wirtz fires GM Bob Murray, demotes Lorne Mollekin to assistant coach, and brings 63-year-old Bob Pulford out of semi-retirement as interim GM and coach. Mike Smith is named manager of hockey operations. Hall of Fame center Stan Mikita recovers from an aneurysm. Smith sends veteran defensemen Sylvain Cote and Dave Manson to Dallas in return for defenseman Kevin Dean, center Derek Plante, and a second-round draft choice. Bob Probert tops the 3,000 plateau in career penalty minutes. Hawks trade Doug Gilmour and J.P. Dumont to Buffalo for Michal Grosek. Hawks miss playoffs. Pulford insists he will not be back as coach. Tony Amonte leads all Hawks with 43 goals and 84 points. Mollekin is fired at the end of the season.

Blackhawks
Rewarded for Excellence

F ROM Pierre Pilote's three Norris wins to Eddie Belfour's pair of Vezinas, the Blackhawks have been celebrated for their winning tradition for years.

Hart Trophy
(most valuable player to his team)

Max Bentley — 1946
Al Rollins — 1954
Bobby Hull — 1965, 1966
Stan Mikita — 1967, 1968

— **Lionel Conacher** was runner-up to Aurel Joliat in 1934
— **Paul Thompson** was runner-up to Eddie Shore in 1938
— **Doug Bentley** was runner-up to Bill Cowley in 1943
— **Al Rollins** was runner-up to Gordie Howe in 1953
— **Bobby Hull** was runner-up to Gordie Howe in 1960 and Jean Beliveau in 1964
— **Stan Mikita** was runner-up to Gordie Howe in 1963
— **Tony Esposito** was runner-up to Bobby Orr in 1970

Art Ross Trophy
(leading point scorer)

Doug Bentley — 1943
Max Bentley — 1946, 1947
Roy Conacher — 1949
Bobby Hull — 1960, 1962, 1966
Stan Mikita — 1964, 1965, 1967, 1968

— **Dick Irvin** was runner-up to Bill Cook in 1927
— **Doug Bentley** was runner-up to Herb Cain in 1944 and
Roy Conacher in 1949
— **Bobby Hull** was runner-up to Stan Mikita in 1964 and 1967
and Phil Esposito in 1969
— **Stan Mikita** was runner-up to Bobby Hull in 1966

Lady Byng Memorial Trophy
(sportsmanship and gentlemanly conduct)

Doc Romnes — 1936
Max Bentley — 1943
Clint Smith — 1944
Bill Mosienko — 1945
Ken Wharram — 1964
Bobby Hull — 1965
Stan Mikita — 1967, 1968

— **Dick Irvin** was runner-up to Billy Burch in 1927
— **Clint Smith** was runner-up to Toe Blake in 1946

James Norris Memorial Trophy
(best defenseman)

Pierre Pilote — 1963, 1964, 1965
Doug Wilson — 1982
Chris Chelios — 1993, 1996

— **Pierre Pilote** was runner-up to Doug Harvey in 1962,
Jacques Laperriere in 1966, and Harry Howell in 1967
— **Chris Chelios** was runner-up to Paul Coffey in 1995

Frank J. Selke Trophy
(best defensive forward)

Troy Murray — 1986
Dirk Graham — 1991

Calder Memorial Trophy
(top rookie)

Mike Karakas — 1936
Cully Dahlstrom — 1938
Ed Litzenberger — 1955
Bill Hay — 1960
Tony Esposito — 1970
Steve Larmer — 1983
Ed Belfour — 1991

— **George Gee** was runner-up to Edgar Laprade in 1946
— **Bobby Hull** was runner-up to Frank Mahovlich in 1958
— **Ed Van Impe** was runner-up to Bobby Orr in 1967
— **Eric Daze** was runner-up to Daniel Alfredsson in 1996

Vezina Trophy
(best goaltender)

Charlie Gardiner — 1932, 1934
Lorne Chabot — 1935
Glenn Hall — 1963
Glenn Hall and Denis DeJordy — 1967
Tony Esposito — 1970
Tony Esposito and Gary Smith — 1972
Ed Belfour — 1991, 1993

— **Charlie Gardiner** was runner-up to Tiny Thompson
in 1930 and Roy Worters in 1931
— **Mike Karakas** was runner-up to Tiny Thompson in 1936
— **Glenn Hall** was runner-up to Jacques Plante in 1960,
Johnny Bower in 1961, Charlie Hodge in 1964, and
Gump Worsley and Charlie Hodge in 1966
— **Tony Esposito** was runner-up to Ed Giacomin and
Gilles Villemure in 1971
— **Ed Belfour** was runner-up to Dominik Hasek in 1995

Bill Masterton Trophy
(for perseverance, sportsmanship, and dedication to hockey)

Pit Martin — 1970

Jack Adams Award
(coach of the year)

Orval Tessier — 1983

William M. Jennings Trophy
(goaltender(s) with fewest goals against)

Ed Belfour — 1991, 1993, 1995

— **Ed Belfour** was runner-up to Patrick Roy in 1992

Blackhawks in the Hall of Fame

Name	Year Elected	With Blackhawks
Charlie Gardiner	1945	1927–34
Howie Morenz	1945	1934–36
Mickey MacKay	1952	1926–28
Herb Gardiner	1958	1928–28
George Hay	1958	1926–27
Dick Irvin	1958	1926–29, 1930–31, 1955–56
Duke Keats	1958	1927–29
Hugh Lehman	1958	1926–28
George "Buck" Boucher	1960	1931–32
Charlie Conacher	1961	1947–50
James D. Norris	1962	1952–66
Barney Stanley	1962	1927–28
Major Frederic McLaughlin	1963	1926–44
Tommy Gorman	1963	1933–34
Earl Seibert	1963	1936–45
Ebbie Goodfellow	1963	1950–52
Doug Bentley	1964	1939–44, 1945–52
"Black Jack" Stewart	1964	1950–52
Bill Mosienko	1965	1941–55
Max Bentley	1966	1940–47
Frank Brimsek	1966	1949–50
Ted Lindsay	1966	1957–60
Sid Abel	1969	1952–54
Babe Dye	1970	1926–28
Bill Gadsby	1970	1946–54
Arthur Wirtz	1971	1952–83
Billy Burch	1974	1933
Art Coulter	1974	1931–36

Tommy Ivan	1974	1954–99
Carl Voss	1974	1937–38
Glenn Hall	1975	1957–67
Pierre Pilote	1975	1955–68
Bill Wirtz	1976	1954–present
Bobby Orr	1979	1976–78
Harry Lumley	1980	1950–52
Allan Stanley	1981	1954–56
Emile Francis	1982	1947–48
Bobby Hull	1983	1957–72
Stan Mikita	1983	1958–80
Phil Esposito	1984	1963–67
John Mariucci	1985	1940–48
Bert Olmstead	1985	1948–50
Rudy Pilous	1985	1958–63
Tony Esposito	1988	1969–84
Bud Poile	1990	1947–48
Clint Smith	1991	1943–47
Bob Pulford	1991	1977–present
Lionel Conacher	1994	1933–34
Harry Watson	1994	1954–57
Al Arbour	1996	1958–61
Roy Conacher	1998	1947–52
Michel Goulet	1998	1990–94

Retired numbers

1	Glenn Hall
9	Bobby Hull
21	Stan Mikita
35	Tony Esposito